GW00708118

A GLOSSARY
OF HIMALAYAN BUDDHISM

A Glossary of HIMALAYAN BUDDHISM

Jagadish Chandra Regmi

Illustrated by Uday Shankar

Nirala

Nirala Publications
G.P.O. Box 394
Nawab Ka Chauraha, Ghat Gate
Jaipur 302 001 (India)

Postal Address:
2595 Kucha Challan
Darya Ganj New Delhi 110 002.

First Edition 1994

ISBN-81-85693-28-5

Cover Design and Illustrations : Uday Shankar

Typesetting at
Micro Tech Printage
Darya Ganj, New Delhi

Printed at
S.S. Enterprises
Darya Ganj, New Delhi

Dr. Jagadish Chandra Regmi (1944) received his education mainly at Banaras Hindu Vishwavidyalya, Varanasi where he received his Master's in Ancient Indian History, Culture and Archaeology in 1965 and his doctoral degree in 1970 under the Colombo Plan. Since then, Dr. Regmi has been involved in various research pursuits including the compilation and publication of the socio-historical journal, *Nepal Antiquary*. In 1979 he received *Sajha Prakashan Award* for his outstanding research output in the field of Nepalese history, archaeology and culture and in 1992 Royal Nepal Academy bestowed upon him the most prestigious *Tribhuvan Prajna Puruskar* of Rs. 1.50 lakhs.

His published works include, *Saat Sahityik Ra Aitihasik Abhilekh* (Nepali, 1968), *Nepal Ko Sanskshipta Itihas* (Nepali, 1969), *Lichhavi Sanskriti* (Nepali, 1969), *Nepal Ko Dharmik Itihas* (Nepali, 1976), *Prachin Nepal Ko Rajanitik Itihas* (Nepali, 1978) *Nepal and Her Friends* (1978) *Shahakalin Kala Ra Vastukala* (Nepali, 1980), *Temples of Kathmandu* (1971) *Nepali Adhyayan* (Two Parts, 1979), *Nepalayan* (Two Parts, 1979), *Nepala Ko Vaidhanik Parampara* (1980), *Nepala Ko Aitihasik Bhugol*, (1981), *Prachin Nepali Sanskriti*, (1983), *Royal Palace Complex of Kathmandu* (1992) and *Kumari of Kathmandu*, (1992).

Currently, Dr. Regmi lectures at the History Department of Tribhuvan University, Kathmandu.

Preface

Why Buddhism?

Politically our country Nepal may appear an insignificant geographical stretch intervening two giant countries. Even economically the country has not been able to do any major achievement to prove its own capability. But the country can boast to have retained most vivid example of religious cultures since the historical times. Buddhism is one such culture which has been preserved more or less intact in this country to exemplify the real zeal of the people in spiritual and cultural traditions.

Though our country has awakened academically, the vast subject of socio-cultural-spiritual study and advanced research is certainly missing. Regarding the advanced and scrutinised study of Nepali Buddhism, the book proposes an ambitious programme.

A Buddhist Centre

A Buddhist centre in Nepal has become a necessity because nowhere in the world such an institution has been known to exist to coordinate among the Buddhist peoples of many countries and research institutions dedicated to this cause. I propose to establish a Buddhist centre to work for the said object. This book may be taken as a first step towards the realisation of the dream of establishing a Buddhist centre.

Hereafter, the author proposes to produce the following works on Nepali Buddhism:

1. Sources to Nepal Buddhism
2. Buddhist Sculptures of Nepal
3. Buddhist Inscriptions
4. Buddhist Shrines
5. Buddhist Biharas
6. Buddhist Rituals
7. Buddhist Kings of Nepal
8. Buddhist Education
9. Buddhist Geography
10. Buddhist People
11. Chronology of Buddhist Sects
12. Buddhist Literature
13. Buddhist Tantra
14. Yoga of the Buddhists
15. Lamaism in Nepal

After completing these works, I hope to produce works related to Buddhist literature, philosophical aspects and Buddhism in various countries. I will need vast resources to complete these works. Hence a request to all lovers of the subject to come forward to cooperate is made here.

In this work I have collected only those references on Nepali Buddhism which are legendary in form. Only here and there the readers will find other types of references which are known from different sources. Therefore, this volume contains a preliminary study of Nepal Buddhism.

Buddhism vs Hinduism

Sanatanist Hindus find the extension of the original Vedic Hinduism in Buddhism and take Buddha as the ninth incarnation of Lord Vishnu. They put forward some medieval instances where the Lord is described as an incarnation of Lord Vishnu. In his *Dasha Avatara Stotram* Shankaracharya has included Lord Buddha among Lord Vishnu's incarnations. A 12th century poet Jaya Deva devoted to Vaishnavism also refers to the same fact. Another famous poet and critic Kshemendra has given a separate chapter on Lord Buddha as the ninth incarnation of Lord Vishnu in his work, *Dash Avatara.*

But in Nepal, Buddhism stands in a little different position. The Buddhism followed by the Newars appears more influenced by Shaivism. This fact may be found exampled in the cult of Ashta Vaitaragas according to which the eight famous Shivaligas of the Nepal Valley are also identified as Bodhisattwas. Lord Pashupati himself is taken as the Naga Lokeshwara by the Buddhists. Other numerous instances support the above stated view. Newar Buddhists worship in Shaivite and Vaishnavite shrines and do not differentiate them from their own religion. But at the same time they have maintained obscure Buddhist rituals to prove that the religion still stands distinct.

Even Lamaistic Nepalese Buddhists share the Newar Buddhist's attitude in venerating Narayana and Pashupati. Lord Muktinath is also venerated by them who is otherwise known as Narayana.

Tantra in China

Since the institution of Mahayana Buddhism early form of Buddhist Tantra appeared in the scene. Mahayana found a vast empire from Mongolia to China and Tibet as its followers. Later Tibet excelled in Buddhism and impressed upon China and Mongolia. Since Tibet had already developed Mantrayana and Vajrayana in proficiency, the Tantra became famous in China and Mongolia also. This way Tantrik form of Buddhism was prevalent among the Chinese Buddhists. A serious research is needed to elaborate this topic.

Lamaism in Nepal

Northern and Eastern Asian countries had promoted an esteemed Buddhism in their own form. Buddhism was at its zenith in the 7th century A.D. in those territories. Nepal and India had helped to propagate and establish Buddhism in Tibet. Later China and Mongolia had greatly influenced Buddhism in Tibet. Hence, the Lamaism was formed in that country. Nepal Buddhists also came in direct contact with Lamaism in Tibet. Even at home the Khasa Malla rulers of Jumla were Lamaistic Buddhists. Since that time the whole length of Nepalese Himalayan parts became converted into Lamaism mainly because the people had migrated here along with the Lamaistic religion. Northern peoples Mugalis, Bhotes, Thakalis, Gurungs, Magars, Tamangs and Sherpas are the followers of the same sect and were divided into different sub-sects.

There are many Lamaistic centres in Nepal in

the Himalayan range including Swayambhu and Bauddha. There are several Lamaistic Gumbas where Lama incarnates continue their religious activities.

Nepalese Kings and Buddhism

Since the time of King Brisha Deva of Circa 300 A.D. Nepalese kings appear to have approved the socio-cultural importance of Buddhism. Therefore we find numerous historical evidences which prove Nepalese Kings' patronization of Buddhism. This attitude of Nepalese kings has certainly enhanced the Buddhist activities and built temples, Biharas, Gombas and antiquities.

That's why the Buddhists in a special way exhibit their devotion towards kingship. They have also developed several rituals when the King must be invited as the Almighty God in the human form. The Newars continue such rituals till today

Kathmandu **-Jagadish Chandra Regmi**

Contents

A Glossary of Himalayan Buddhism

Adi Buddha, Swayambhu

The Vamshavali states that the lotus seed that had been sown brought forth a lotus flower, in the middle of which Swayambhu, light from Aknisht Bhuvan (heaven), appeared on the Ashwin Shukla Purnima day in the Satya Yuga (Wright, p. 50).

Krakucchanda Buddha is said in the genealogical work to have seen Guhyeshwari in the form of the Swayambhu light (Wright, p. 52).

In the genealogical work we find Shakya Simha Buddha visiting Swayambhu Stupa and praising its sanctity (Wright, p. 73). This probably suggests that the original Swayambhu light is not related to Buddhism.

Bishwarupa Swayambhu

Manjushri Bodhisattwa, as recorded in the genelogical work (Wright, p. 51) having drying the lake, saw the Swayambhu in the form of Bishwarupa on the Kartik Purnima day. He meditated on and worshipped Swayambhu in the centre of the lotus flower whose root was at Guhyeshwari.

King Prachanda Deva of Bengal who became a mendicant after coming to Nepal and called as

Shantikara first and later Shanta Shri Acharya had built the first ever stone chaitya and temple over the Swayambhu light in the beginning of the Kali Yuga, as the genealogical work states (Wright, p. 55).

The Shiva Linga type stone Chaityas of later period seen anywhere in Kathmandu Valley probably relate to the belief that the Swayambhu is in the form of supernatural light similar to that of Pashupati.

The Tibetans call the Swayambhu Stupa by their own Tibetan name Phakpa Singkiun *(Nangba Sange, p. 111).*

Colonel Santa Bir Lama quotes Tibetan sources according to which the Swayambhu Stupa is called Goma Salagendha (Nangba Sange, pp. 80-81). The same source further states that Sange or Thousand Buddhas were created in the form of a lotus flower. `The petals will become Bodhisattwas' was predicted by Lord Buddha to Sariyan and Kungawa.

In the courtyard of Swayambhu Stupa we find stone images of Hanuman and Shiva-Parvati apparently for worshipping. Such instances prove the religious character of the Kathmandu Valley.

Adinath, Chobhar

Since on the Ashwin Shukla Purnima (Kojagrata Purnima) day Buddhist mela for worshipping Adinath of Chobhar begins. Adinath is believed to bless good health and cure tuberculosis and mental sickness.

Agam Digi

Agam Digi is a secret shrine of Newar Buddhists where Vajrayanic mysterious rituals are performed.

One Abhayaraja is recorded in the genealogy to have built an Agama where he had placed an image of Bidyadhari Devi, who is supposed to be a handmaid of Maha Buddha (of Buddha Gaya) (Wright, p. 139).

Ak Bahal

One ancient King Narendra Deva is described in the genealogical work to have renounced the worldly affairs and lived in a Bihar which he had built and named Alag Bahal or Aka Bahal (Wright, p. 93). The Bihar is in Bhaktapur.

Aknishta Bhuvana

The name of the heaven from where the Swayambhu light had come to appear on the lotus flower in the Naga Hrada lake (Wright, p. 50).

Arniko

The famous medieval Nepali artist who had contributed in the field of Buddhist art in Tibet and China.

On Arniko's artistic contributions in Tibet and China I quote here a short but important article written by a Chinese scholar Mr. Hai Lan (Arniko's Architectural Legacy, *China Daily*, quoted in *The Rising Nepal*, November 27, 1981):

Arniko's Architectural Legacy By Hai Lan

> "Seven centuries ago, a 17-year-old Nepali artisan named Arniko climbed over the Himalaya, crossed the Yellow River and came to Beijing, then called Dadu (Great Capital). He went to work

for the Yuan Dynasty (1271-1368) court and died in China.

Today's Beijing would be unrecognizable to Arniko, but he would see at least one familiar sight—the White Dagoba he designed in the city's western district. One of the oldest standing structures in the city, it remains a striking feature of Beijing's skyline despite 700 years of erosion by wind and rain.

Yuan Dynasty Records describe Arniko as an accomplished architect, painter, sculptor and mechanical engineer. He is among the few foreigners whose biography can be found in Chinese imperial history books. The White Dagoba was built under his supervision from 1271 to 1279. Renovated in 1980, it is now open to tourists.

In sharp contrast to the traditional Chinese buildings with upturned caves which surround Arniko's creation, and the modern high-rises in the neighborhood, the 51.3 metre-high Dagoba has the simple and lyrical lines of South Asian architecture.

Located inside the Miaoying Monastery, the dagoba is comprised of three parts: a nine metre-high foundation, a body, the shape of an inverted bowl bound with seven iron hoops, and a towering golden pinnacle. Below the gilded tip is a canopy hung with 36 bronze bells which jingle in the breeze.

Arniko undertook the project for Emperor Kublai Khan, founder of the Yuan Dynasty. Expanding the bounds of the empire of his grand father, Genghis Khan, Kublai had moved southward from the Mongolian plateau to conquer the Southern Song Dynasty. He built the new capital of Dadu on a stretch of wilderness in north China.

Kublai Khan

Eceectic in his religious views, Kublai venerated Lamaisem, a branch of Buddhism, believing it would help consolidate his rule. He ordered Phagaspa, the governor of Tibet, to build a golden dagoba in Tibet. Phagaspa turned to the King of Nepal for skilled craftsmen.

Yuan Dynasty chronicles record that the king chose Eighty artisans and asked them to nominate a leader. None dared assume the position until 17-year-old Arniko stepped forward. The king said that he was too young, and Arniko responded, "I am young, but I am aspiring". So he got the job.

Under Arniko's leadership, the golden Dagoba in Tibet went up within two years. Phagaspa was so impressed by the young man's talents that he brought Arniko to Dadu to call on Kublai Khan. First, Phagaspa personally shaved Arniko's head and accepted him as a disciple of Lamaism.

The chronicles record that when Arniko was brought before the emperor, Kublai asked, "Are you not afraid to come to the great empire?"

Arniko answered, "A sage takes people

everywhere as his own children. Now that I am before my father, there is no reason to be afraid."

To test Arniko, Kublai asked him to repair a damaged bronze figure used for acupuncture. The task took Arniko's four years. When the emperor saw the mended joints, arteries and veins of the figure, he was delighted. From then on, he entrusted Arniko with building temples and pagodas and making Buddhist statues.

By 1271, Dadu was prospering, and life was relatively peaceful after years of war. Pleased with his achievements and feeling he owed them in part to Lamaism, he asked Arniko to build a dagoba in the capital. So construction of the White Dagoba and the monastery around it began.

Arniko was appointed chief artisan of the Yuan court two years later, and by the time the dagoba was done he had been promoted to minister in charge of imperial construction. His Nepali wife was brought to China, and the emperor granted him the granddaughter of a Song prince as his second wife.

The White Dagoba was the tallest structure in the Yuan capital. An inscription written for Arniko's tomb-stone says that when it was completed, "Mysterious and auspicious light from the dagoba rose to the sky. The emperor went to see it and was overjoyed."

In addition to the dagobas in Tibet and Dadu, Arniko designed an even larger one on Wutai Mountain in Shanxi Province, a holy Buddhist site. He also designed instruments for astronomy, painted pictures for the royal family, and modelled Buddhist images, one with a thousand eyes and a thousand hands.

Arniko married 10 Chinese women and left behind 14 children. His two eldest sons became architects and sculptors. In 1307, he died at the age of 63. He was buried on Fragrant Hill in the northwest suburb of Dadu. His grave commanded a view of the city where he had spent most of his life.

Although the tomb itself is yet to be discovered, the inscription on Arniko's tombstone can be found in a collection of classical essays by Chen Jufu, "Snow building Writing". "His major achievements include three dagobas, nine monasteries, two ancestral temples and one palace," it says, "as well as innumerable sculptures, statues, paintings and utensils used in the imperial court". (Courtesy: *China Daily*) November 27, 198.

Anandadi Lokeshwar

According to the genealogy some people had migrated to Chobhar where they erected an image of Lokeshwar naming it Anandadi Lokeshwar or the Giver of happiness to the people of the world (Wright, p. 68). The deity is also called Adinatha. It is also said there that some Bhikshus had gone to live there to live on alms and those who were householders paid there recluse brethren money for performing the Lokeshwar jatra (festival). (Also see Adinath Chobhar).

Ashoka Sends Missionaries to The Himalayas

The great King Ashoka is reported in the text of Mahavamsha to have sent nine missionary teams to various countries, one of them being led by Majjhima to the Himalayan region. (The age of Imperial Unity, p. 84). The said team might have

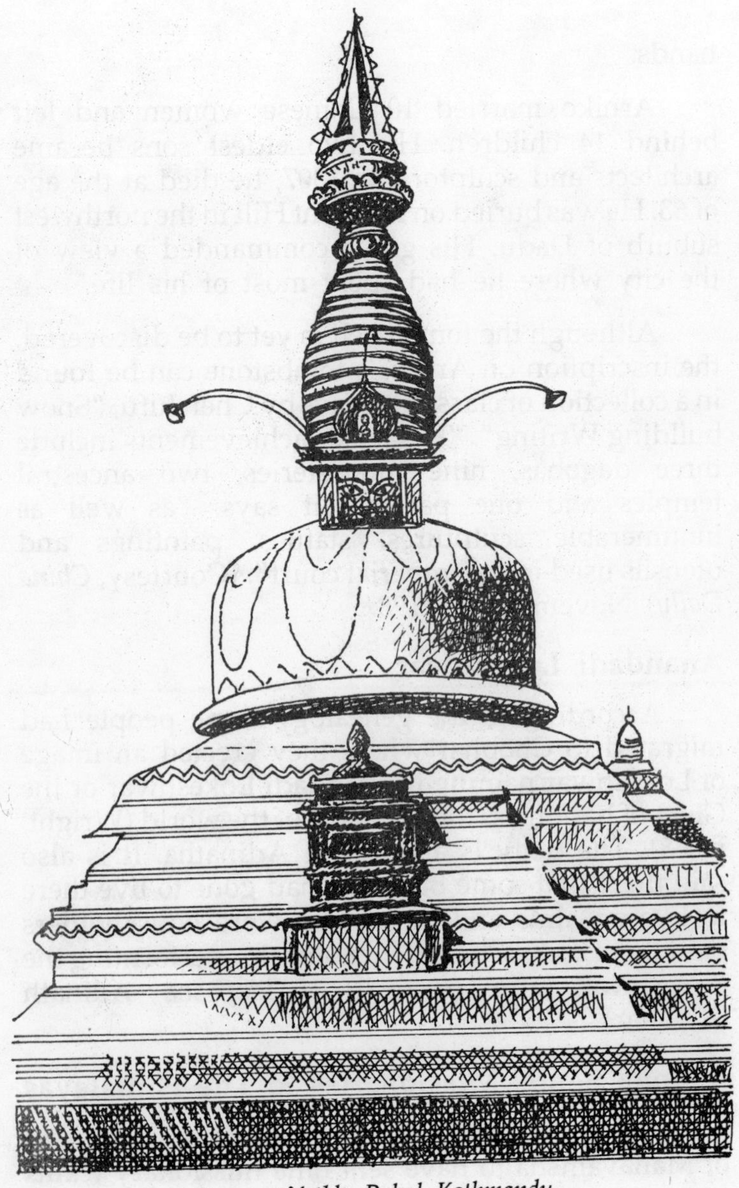

Stupa at Yetkha Bahal, Kathmandu

Aryabalikiteshor

visited Nepal also.

Ashoka Stupas of Patan

In one genealogical work we find mention of the origin of the four so-called Ashoka Stupas of Patan (Yogi Debinath Devamala Vamshavali, p. 71). According to the said source during King Bira Deva's time one merchant named Bundar had gone to the ocean and had brought hundred crore worth of jewels. After selling those jewels for hundred crore of money he returned and built a Thulo Chaitya. Putting a crore of money under it he established it on Magha Shukla Panchami in Kaligata Year 3608-9 (A.D. 507?). Similarly the following 4 chaityas were built (by the merchant Bundar himself?)

1. Thulo chaitya of Lagankhel.
2. Thulo chaitya of Pulchok.
3. Thulo chaitya of the place Teta.
4. Thulo chaitya outside the Yape Bahi.

In the later type of genealogical work we find King Ashoka building the four Stupas each of which was founded on the anniversary of the commencement of one of the four Yugas (Wright, pp. 77-78).

Ashoka Chaitya	**Yuga, Commorated**
1. Yampi Bihar	Kali Yuga
2. Lagankhel	Satya Yuga
3. Imadol (South of Imadol Chaitya)	Treta Yuga

The genealogy also records that one Sunaya Shri Mishra Brahman of Kapilbastu had put a crystal jewel in one of the four Ashokan Stupas and had repaired all the four.

Ashoka's Visit to Lumbini

In B.C. 249 Magadha's Emperor Ashoka had visited Lumbini, the Birth place of Lord Buddha. In the Lumbini pillar inscription Emperor Ashoka states that he had set up this pillar in the Lumbini village at the very spot where Shakyamuni was born.

Ashoka's Visit to the Valley

The genealogical work (Wright, pp. 74-75) describes Ashoka's visit to the valley during Kirati King Sthunko's time. The Magadhan King is said there to have obtained his spiritual guide Bhikshu Upa Gupta's permission for the pilgrimage, accompanied by his family and followed by a large number of his subjects. King Ashoka is recorded there to have visited every holy place, and bathed in every sacred water, went to Swayambhu, Guhyeshwari, and eight Buddha Bitaragas or chaityas. He also built there several chaityas. The legend also records that Ashoka gave his daughter Charumati to one Devapala in marriage. During their return to Magadha a child Mahipana was born to Ashoka from his Queen Tikhya Lakshmi.

Ashta Matrikas Worshipped by the Buddhists

A peculiar instance is found in the genealogical work that Patan King Shri Nivasa saw one night at a window on the eastern side of his palace the Ashta Matrika goddesses entering and after dancing vanished again. The King became pleased, and calling into his presence Bauddhacharyas of Buya Bihar Nakabahil Tol and Onkuli Bihar and ordered them by turns to worship the Ashta Matrikas in their houses during Ashwin Navaratri, and to bring them to dance at the palace. The cost was defrayed by the palace. This custom is observed to the present day (Wright, p. 167).

Ashwin Shukla Purnima

The memorable day when Swayambhu light appeared in the middle of the lotus flower whose seed had been sown by Bipashwi Buddha in the Naga Hrada lake (Wright, p. 50).

On the Ashwin Shukla Purnima (or Kojagrat Purnima) (October 24, 1983) day Buddhists also offer umbrellas to the famous chaityas within the valley.

Bagmati River, Origin

Krakucchanda Buddha who is said to have visited the valley in Treta Yuga is credited in the genealogical work to have created the Ganga river, later called as Bagmati (Wright, p. 52). It is stated in the said source that Krakucchanda Buddha ascended the high mountain in north of the valley and made his abode there. When he began to anoint and sprinkle water to his disciples [Bhikshus] he could not find water there then he prayed to Swayambhu and Guhyeshwari to get water and thrust his thumb into the mountain and made a hole through which Ganga Devi appeared in corporal form and offered handful of water to the Buddha and then changing her form into water ran out of the mountain on the Mesha Sankranti(Vaishakh Sankranti) day and became known as Bagmati.

Bahi and Bahal

According to the traditions of Newar Buddhists the Bahis are those Buddhist monasteries where

Brahmachari (celibate) Bhikshus live, while in Bahals married Buddhist families live.

Bajrapani Bodhisattwa

The Kumbheshvara or Sarveshvara of Patan is included by *Swayambhu Purana* in the Ashta Vaitaraga list of deities. There Shiva Kumbheshvara or Sarveshvara is taken as Vajrapani Bodhisattwa who adores himself with Damaru, Vajra, Ghanta, Trishul and tiger skin. Akshobhya Tathagata is seated on his crown. One Sarvapal Vaidya had first got sight of the god (*Hemaraja Shakya Kumbheshvara Itihasa*, Sahu Shri Bekhanath Shrestha, Lalitpur Kobahal, VS. 2018, pp.1-4)

Bandas

About the social and religious status of the Bajracharyas King Jayasthiti Malla's five legal councillors had to consider that the Bandyas had been converted in the Treta Yuga, by Krakucchanda Buddha, from the Brahman and Kshatriya castes, and had become Bhikshus, and that these again had been made householders by Shankaracharya. It is, moreover, written in the scriptures that first of all one should live as a Brahmachari and read all the scriptures, secondly, that he should live as a Grihastha (householder), thirdly, that he should accept Pravrajya Vrata, and live in the woods as a Banaprastha Bhikshu, and fourthly, that he should return to the life of a Grihastha, and instruct sons and grandsons, living himself in a state of Nirbritti (free from worldly cares). He who does all this receives the title of Buddha (Bauddha) or Bajracharya Arhat Bhikshu (Wright, p. 125). But Shankaracharya had forced these people to change from Bhikshus to Grihasthas without passing through the four different kinds of lives, and being thus fathers of families, they were obliged to attend to worldly affairs, but still they were respected by the four castes. Hence, it was determined to class them as Brahmans and Kshatriyas, their customs and ceremonies being the same. Bandyas, therefore, are like Sannyasis who are all of one class without distinction of caste. (Wright, pp. 125-6).

Patan King Siddhi Nara Simha Malla is recorded in the genealogical work (Wright, p.159) that seeing that there were not carpenters enough in the city of Patan, he made Bandyas take up trade, and assigned Guthis to the Naikyas (Headmen) to give them a feast on a certain day of every year.

King Bhupalendra is stated in the genealogy to have instituted the Jatra of Sweta Binayaka, and the Guthi or lands assigned for its support, were given in charge to the Bandas of Chabahil (in Ca. 1693 A.D.) (Wright, p. 150).

During the Chinese invasion of A.D. 1792 Bahadur Shah, the then Regent, had employed one Lakhya Banda of Bhinkshe Bahal to perform Purashchrana (Wright, p. 177).

Hodgson has described the Bandyas in detail as quoted below:

> The Bandyas are divided into two classes, those who follow the Vahyacharya, and those who adopt the Abhayantara-charya words equivalent to the Grihastha ashrama and Vairagi ashrama of the Brahmanas. The first class is denominated Bhikshu; the second Vajra Acharya.

The Bhikshu cannot marry but the Vajra Acharya is a family man. The latter is sometimes called, in the vernacular tongue of the Newars, Gubhal, which is not a Sanskrit word. Besides this distinction into monastic and secular orders, the Bandyas are again divided, according to the scriptures, into five classes:

(i) Arhat

(ii) Bhiksu

(iii) Shravaka

(iv) Chailaka

(v) Vajra Acharya

The Arhat is he who is perfect himself, and can give perfection to others, who eats what is offered to him, but never asks for anything.

The Bhiksu is he who assumes a staff and beggar's dish (bhiksari and Pinda Patra) sustains himself by alms, and devotes his attention solely to the contemplation (dhyana) of Adi Buddha without ever meddling with worldly affairs.

The Shravaka is he who devotes himself to hearing the Bauddha scriptures read or reading them to others; these are his sole occupations, and he is sustained by the small presents of his audiences.

The Chailaka is he who contents himself with such a portion of clothes (chilaka) as barely suffices to cover his nakedness, rejecting anything more as superfluous. The Bhiksu and the Chailaka very nearly resemble each other, and both (and the Arhat also) are bound to practice celibacy.

The Vajra Acharya is he who has a wife and children, and devotes himself to the active ministry of Buddhism.

Such is the account of the five classes found in the scriptures, but there are no races of them in Nepal.

In Nepal at present the Bandyas are divided popularly into Vajra Acharya, Shakya Vamshi, Bhiksu or Bikhu and Chiva-bare. The last derive their name from living in a Vihar which has a chaitya, Vulgo Chiva, in it. Others say that Chiva or Chivakbare is a corruption of a chailaka Bandya potius, Bandyas wearing the Chivara, a part of the monastic dress, a sense which would make the term signify Bandyas adhering to their vows.

All the Nepali Bauddhamargis are married. They pursue the business of the world, and seldom think of the injunctions of their religion. The Tantras and Dharanis, which ought to be read for their own salvation, they do only for the increase of their stipend and from a greedy desire of money. This division into five classes is according to the scriptures, but there is a popular division according to Vihars, and these Vihars being very numerous, the separate congregations of the Bandyas, have been thus greatly multiplied. Some years ago there were 5000 Bandyas in the valley of Nepal out of a population of some 250000.

In Patan alone there are 15 Vihars. A temple to Adi Buddha, or to the five Dhyani Buddhas, called a chaitya, is utterly distinct from the Vihar, and of the form of a heap of rice or Dhanyarasyakar. But the temples of Shakya and the other of the 'Sapta Buddha Manusi', as well as those of other chief saints and leaders of Buddhism are called Vihars.

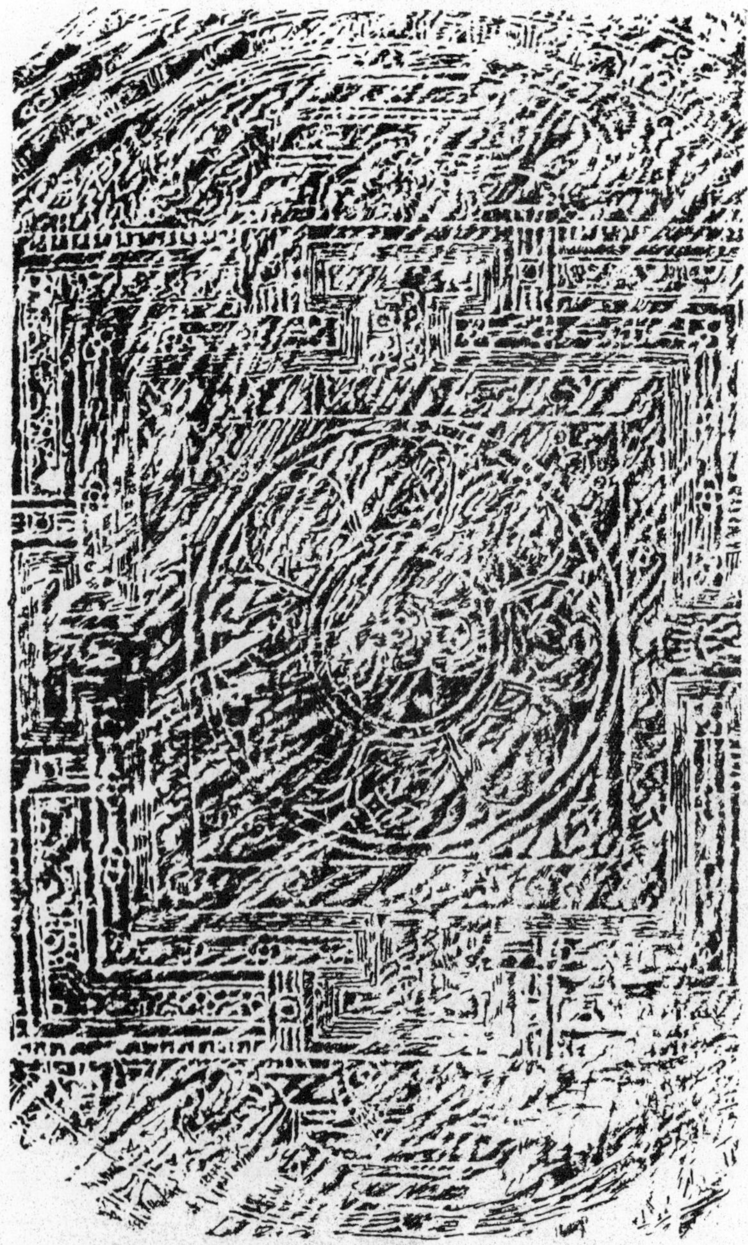

Mandala, Swayambhu, Eastern Courtyard

Famous Vihars of Patan

The names of some of the 15 Vihars of Patan are as follows:

1. Tankal Vihar
2. Tu Vihar
3. Hak Vihar
4. Bhu Vihar
5. Haran Varna Mahavihar (Kon Vihar)
6. Rudra Varna Mahavihar (Uku Vihar)
7. Bhiksu Vihar
8. Shakya Vihar
9. Guhya Vihar
10. Shi Vihar
11. Dhom Vihar
12. Un Vihar, etc.

In short, if any Bandyas die, and his son erect a temple in his name, such structure may be called one's (after his name) Vihar. With this distinction, however, that a temple to an eminent saint is denominated Maha Vihar - one to an ordinary mortal, simply Vihar. (Hodgson, Essays, 1874, pp. 51-53).

Bandhu Datta Bajracharya

Bandhu Datta is a famous personality in the late period genealogies.

In one type of genealogy (Wright, pp. 91-93) Bandhu Datta occurs as a Bajracharya who after becoming a Bhikshu had returned to the householder's life. After observing great austerities he had achieved an advanced command over Tantrik miracles.

Once Bandhu Datta was roaming in the woods and forests performing all round reciting of Mantras and visiting many holy places. When he returned to his city Bishalnagar, he found that his city was being plundered by enemies. He found King Chandraketu Deba and his wife starving in a room. He then caused Pancha Rashmi Tej (solar spectrum) to emanate from his body and illuminate the room in which the King was lying. The King became surprised at seeing the light, got up and went in search of the light. He then met Bandhu Datta who assured him to put an end of his misfortunes by worshipping deities. Bandhu Datta then invoked and installed Lumadi Mahakali Devi who instantly caused a light to issue from her body. The kings became frightened and restored all the riches carried by them.

Chandraketu Deva's son Narendra Deva is said in the genealogy to have built a Tirtha Bihar and given it to Bandhu Datta. The King sent his second son Ratna Deva to become a student of Bandhu Datta in Tirtha Bihar. Bandhu Datta placed many deities in the Tirtha Bihar. At the north-east corner of Tirtha Bihar, he placed Mahakala which was brought from Tibet.

Bandhu Datta is again described to have taken pains to bring Aryavalokiteshwara Matsyendra Natha into Nepal during King Bara Deva's reign (see Aryavalokiteshwara Matsyendra Natha).

Bandya Gaon

One King Brikhra Deva Varma is said in the genealogy to have placed an image of Pancha Buddha and named the village Bandya gaon (Wright, p. 78). The name of the village, Bande Gaon which is situated near Godabari, also reminds us its Buddhist origin.

Barada, Goddess

Manjushri Bodhisattwa is said in the genealogical work to have placed his consort goddess Barada on the Phullochacha (Phulchoki) mountain top (Wright, p. 51). She is also called as Laksmi or the goddess of riches.

Barahi Devi

When the Stupa of Bauddha was being built by King Mana Deva, it is alleged in the genealogical work (Wright, p. 67) that Goddess Barahi Devi to test the King's devotion came in the shape of a sow and trod on them repeatedly. Then the king inquired who she was, and the Goddess disclosed herself in her true form. The king to pay his gratitude, placed her image at the entrance of the Stupa which contained all other deities.

Basundhara, Goddess

Buddhists worship Basundhara as the representation of mother earth.

On Ashvin Krishna Chaturthi (in 1982 it coincided on September 7) Buddhists in Patan worship the Basundhara goddess at Shri Baccha Mahavihar in Shri Bahal tol locality. On the occasion Buddhist devotees worship and pay homage to most of the Basundhara images installed within the Patan city. It is believed that the goddess gives knowledge, riches, jewels and grains to her devotees.

In the genealogical work Basundhara Devi is stated to have her residence on the Phullochcha or Phulchoki mountain (Wright, p. 65). The goddess is said there to have discovered the Godabari, a most sacred pond in the valley.

The type of Stupa built at Lumbini to commerate Buddha's Birth as according to Tibetan tradition.

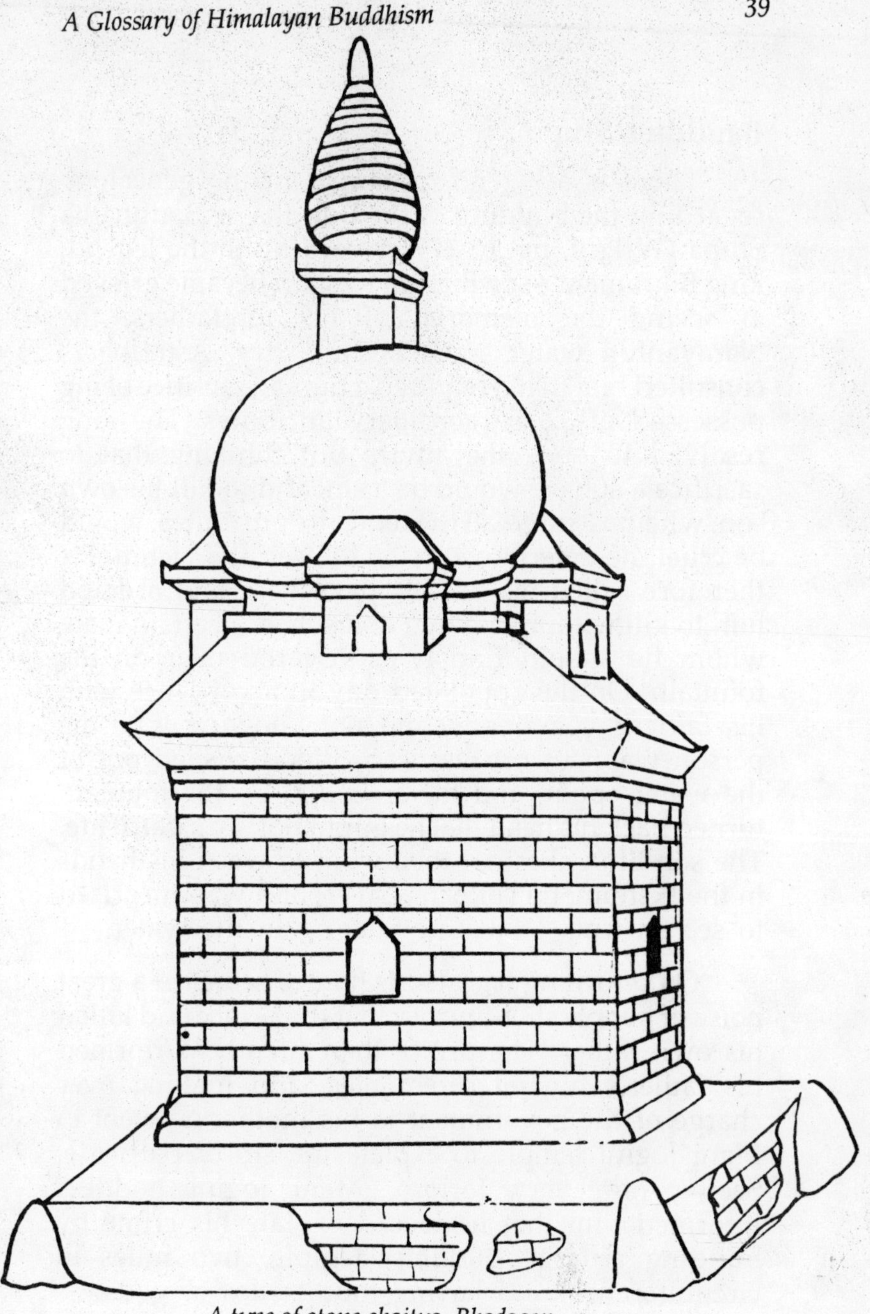

A type of stone chaitya, Bhadgaon

Bauddha Stupa

There is a legend contained in the genealogy regarding the building of the Buddha or Bodhnatha Stupa (Wright, pp. 66-67). According to the legend, king Bikramajit's son Bikram Keshari became grieved at seeing the memorial of his forefathers, the Narayanhiti water spout become dry. Astrologers consulted him that it required a human sacrifice being possessed of 32 extraordinary attributes. The king resolved to obey the advice but thinking that to sacrifice a subject would be a sin, and to kill his own son, who possessed all the requisite attributes, would be cruel, he determined to be himself the victim. He therefore called his son Bhupakeshari, and ordered him to kill without looking at his face, a certain man, whom he should find lying covered over on the fountain. On the appointed day in accordance with his father's commands, and not knowing who the person was, cut off his head. Blood rushed out of the water spout, and the crocodile on the fountain turned back his head that he might not see a patricide. The son Bhupakeshari then went to wash his hands in the Ikshumati (Tukucha) river, and was surprised to see swarms of worms floating in the water.

On returning back to his house, he heard a great noise of people shouting out that the prince had killed his own father. The prince then silently performed his father's funeral ceremonies, and making over charge of the government to his mother,he went to Mani Jogini temple to expiate the sin of patricide. Seeing him very forlorn, Mani Jogini goddess informed him that he would expiate his crime by building a large Buddhist temple, two miles in circumference, and having four circles of gods.

Another version of the story is that it was King Vikmanti who was sacrificed, and that his son Mana Deva was the patricide. The patricide not being able to disengage his hand to which the severed head attached itself, went to Mani Jogini, by whose advice he built the Buddhist temple and then the head became detached, which head (an image of it) is seen at the temple of Mani Jogini.

When Mana Deva started building the Stupa there was a great drought, therefore, the workmen making the bricks could only get water by soaking clothes (in the beds of the streams) and wringing out the moisture. When the bricks were being made, Barahi Devi, to test their strength, came in the shape of a sow and trod on them. This visit being repeated, the king inquired who she was, and the goddess acceeding to his prayer, disclosed herself in her true form to show his gratitude. The king placed her image at the entrance of the Buddhist stupa which contained all the deities. Mana Deva on this occasion composed a special prayer, which is repeated by every Buddhist when performing worship in holy places:

Reverence to Ratna traya I bow
to thy lotus like feet, O Lord !
Thou art Buddha - thine asylum I seek
There are countless merits
in worshipping Buddha
Thou art the master of religion etc.

According to Tibetan tradition, the Lama of Tibet, having died, became incarnate, and lived again as the King of Nepal, who built the Stupa, and for this reason the Tibetans hold it in great veneration. (Wright, pp. 66-67, 83).

Colonel Santa Bir Lama presents a legend

relating to the building of the Stupa at Buddha (Nangba Sange, pp. 82-85) from Tibetan sources. According to which the Stupa was called Chyarung Khasyor in Tibetan. The legend gives credit to one lady named Dicchyokpa (Machyazima) for its building. In her former birth she was a supernatural nymph who had to be born in Nepal in an ordinary family when her merits were finished. She was married to four husbands successively when they had died one after another. She had given birth to four sons from each husband, named Najebu, Phakjepu, Khijepu and Chyajepu. All these sons wanted to build a Stupa for which the mother Michyajima acquired land from the King of Nepal and started building the Stupa. But the mother died after four years during the progress of the Stupa, therefore the sons completed it in more three years. Thus the Stupa was completed in seven years time. When the Stupa was being commissioned all supernaturals represented there symbolically.

Newars call it Khasti chaitya. In Newari language Khasu means dew and its full name is Khasuti or Khasati or Khasti chaitya.

A miraculous event related to the Stupa of Bauddha is recorded in the Gorkha Patra of A.D. 1907 (VS. 1964 Sharavan 21 Gate Somavar, quoted in Gorkha Patra, Shravan, 32, 2037, August 16,1980). The said source states that on the 4th of the month of Shravan water poured from the southern part of the Stupa at 9-30 morning time. Three Bhote women could get the water and after that it stopped. The water had come from a hole which was meant to ooze water. It was believed that water oozed from that hole in every 12 years.

Bhairava at Nuwakot

Scholars have suggested that the temple of Bhairava and Bhairavi at Nuwakot and Manakamana were established by Vajrayani Siddhas (DV Vajracharya, T.B. Shrestha - Shahakalka Abhilekh Pt. 1. p. 69). The Vajracharya Priest of Nuwakot Bhairava temple is the teacher of Thapa Magar priest of Manakamana temple.

Bidyadhara Barma Bihar

In the genealogical work we find a legend relating to this Bihar. According to the genealogy (Wright, pp. 106-7) during King Shankara Deva's time some people of a village named Jhul (a place lying between Kirtipur and Matatirtha) had gone to Bengal and lived in the Kaphi city, where several persons returned to Jhul. These men performed Yajna daily in a hollow consecrated place, Yajna Kunda, where perpetual fire was kept alight. He who undertakes this fire worship has to perform the Yajna with his wedded wife sitting by his side, as Shiva and Shakti and it is never performed by a single person. One of these Brahmans, having no lawful wife, took with him a Brahmani widow, named Yashodhara. One day as he was performing the ritual the fire increased, and after burning him up, consumed the whole village. The Brahmani widow Yashodhara fled to Patan with a small model of a chaitya, the book of Prajna-Paramita, written in golden letters in Bikram Sambat 245 i.e. A.D. 188, and her infant son Yashodhara. She repaired the Bihar in Gala Bahal built by Bidyadhara Barma, and placed the model chaitya inside the Bihar. She caused her son Yashodhara, after his Chuda Karma, to be made a Bandya, and in order to conceal this from her relatives, who were

Agnihotris, she did not allow the ceremonies attending the Chuda Karma to be performed in front of the Agni Devatas of the Bihar. To this day the Bandyas of this Bihar follow this custom. In other Bihars the custom is different. Previously this Bihar was called Bidyadhara Barma Sanskarita Maha Bihar, but after the Chuda Karma of Yashodhara it became known as Yashodhara Maha Bihar and also as Buya Bahal (towards west of the Patan Darbar).

Bidyadhari Devi

King Gunakama Deva is described in the genealogy to have erected an image of Bidyadhari Devi who had shown herself in the sky to a Pandit named Bajrapada (Wright, pp. 103-4).

In another instance we find Bidyadhari Devi as a handmaid of Maha Buddha (Wright, p. 139). One Abhayaraj of Patan is said in the same source to have made an Agama (secret shrine) where he had placed an image of Bidyadhari Devi.

Bighnantaka Ganesha

How the Buddhists came to worship Ganesha is recorded in a legend stated by a genealogical work (Wright, p. 68). The legend goes, long ago, when Odiya Acharya invited all gods on a mountain except Ganesha who became offended by this and began to modest the Acharya. Lokeshwara Padmapani then sent Kshiti Garbha Bodhisattwa, who created the god Bighnanataka to protect him from Ganesha's attacks. Ganesha, being foiled in his attempts, submitted to Bighnantaka, who in return said, that from that day any one commencing a work should worship Ganesha, in order to prevent any interruption. For this reason Ganesha is first propitiated before any work is undertaken. After this, Kshiti Garbha went away, leaving his spirit in the chhatra or umbrella established by Odiya Acharya, and this chatra became known as Gandheshwara.

Nepalese Buddhists worship Ganesha at every temple but some Ganesha temples particularly are more closely associated with Buddhists. Shveta Ganesha at Chabel Kathmandu is attached to a Buddhist chaitya which clearly suggests that the Buddhists had installed this image. Similar instance is found at the Mhaipi Ajima shrine in Kathmandu where an image of Buddhist Ganesha is worshipped (cf. Dhana Shamsher J.B. Rana - Kamakala Rahasya, p. 101).

Bikramashila Bihar

A legend is contained in the genealogical work relating to the foundation of the Bikramashila Bihar of Thamel by one merchant Simhala (Wright, pp. 56-57):-

During the reign of Simhaketu, a descendant of Gunakama Deva, there was a virtuous merchant named Simhala. Once he took five hundred merchants and proceeded to Simhala Dwipa (Ceylon). On the way they saw golden chaitya and inspite of Simhala's warning the merchants took away gold from it. After crossing with great difficulty the arm of the ocean, in the passage of which the power of Simhal alone saved them. They met a five hundred and one Rakshasis (orgesses), who, in the form of lovely damsels, enchanted them, and each took one as a companion. The Lokeshwara Aryavalokiteshvara, taking pity on Simhal, appeared in the wick of his lamp, and told him what these damsels were, and that some day they would devour his followers. He added that if he doubted him, he could go to Ashayakot, and, if he wanted to be saved, he should go to the seashore, where on the fourth day he would meet a horse, which, after making obesiance, he should mount and cross the sea.

Simhala went to Ashaya (or Ayasa) Kot in the morning, where he saw all sorts of persons who had lost their limbs, which convinced him of the truth of what he had been told by Lokeshvara. He then collected his five hundred companions, and went to the seashore, where they mounted the horse Balah, which took them across the ocean. Their mistresses (the Rakshasis; pursued them calling them by name.The merchants in spite of the warning of Lokeshvara, looked back, fell from the horse and were devoured by the Rakshasis. Simhal was the only one who arrived safely at home followed by his Rakshasi, who remained outside his house without any notice being taken of her by Simhal.

A rumour regarding a beautiful damsel having reached the ears of the Raja of Sankasya Nagari, he sent for her, and kept her in his palace. One day the Rakshasi flew away to the sky, and summoned her sister Rakshasis who came and destroyed the Raja and all his family.

Simhal, having heard all this,went to the Raja's palace and reciting the Mantras of Lokeshvara, flourished his sword and drove away the Rakshasis. The people then elected him to be their king and he ruled for a long time. He pulled down his own house, and built a Bihar, and consecrated an image of Bodhisattwa.

In consideration of the Rakshasi, who followed

him from Ceylon, having been his mistress, he raised a temple for her worship and assigned land for its support. He having no issue, the dynasty became extinct on his death.

To the Bihar which he had built, he gave the same name that Manjushri gave to the one which he caused to spring up for Dharmashri Mitra viz Bikram Shila Bihar.

The Bikrama Shila Bihar is important in another way that here no Shakya or Vajracharya is associated with it but the Pradhan families living in the locality. It is variously known as Thama Bahil (Tha Bahil), Bhagawan Bahal or Bikramashila Bihar.

Bipaswhi Buddha

In the genealogical work we find a legend relating to Bipashwi Buddha's visit of Kathmandu Valley when it was in the form of a lake. The legend goes thus:

"In Satya Yuga, Bipashwi Buddha came from a city known by the name of Bandhumati, and, having taken up his abode on the mountain to the west of Naga Hrad, sowed a lotus-seed in the tank, on the day of the full moon in the month of Chaitra. Having named the mountain on which he dwelt, Jata Matrochacha, he returned to his former abode (i.e. Bandhumati), leaving on the spot his disciples, to whom he foretold future events. In honour of this circumstance, a mela (or fair) is held on the mountain on the day of the full moon in the month of Chaitra" (Wright, p. 50).

Birupaksha, the legend of

The peculiar legend of Birupaksha is recorded

in the Buddhist style of genealogical work but in modified form (Wright, pp. 60-61).

Only in a footnote on the legend of Birupaksha we find the origin of the custom of decorating Pashupati with a Buddhist head dressing and worshipping on the 8th day of Kartik Sukla (Wright, p. 61). Gunananda, a resident of Patan, who had also probably provided the text of the genealogical work had probably noted that fact.

A similar legend appears to have been prevalent in India as we find it referred to Lama Taranath's history of Buddhism (Journal of Asiatic Society of Bengal, 1895, pp. 61 ff.).

Bishnuksha Bihar or Mayura Barma Bihar

We find a legend regarding the foundation of Mayura Varna or Bishnuksha Bihar of Patan by King Shankara Deva's orders (Wright, p. 83). One Buddhist Brahman Jayashri had refused to become convert to Shaivism on Shankaracharya's advent. He had married a daughter of a Bhikshu of Charumati Bihar who, through fear of Shankaracharya had himself entered into matrimony. King Shankara Deva told him to remain a Bandya, if he did not wish to renounce Buddhism. The king had assured him to build a Bihar in Patan. While they were uncertain where to build the Bihar and where to install the deity a peacock came and alighted on a certain spot, and when this was dug, an image of Bishnu was found and taken out. An image of Shakya Simha Buddha was also installed. The Bihar was named after the Mayura or peacock. Because a Bishnu image was found at the site and it is called Bishnuksha Bihar.

Bishnu Malla Honours Aryavalokiteshwara

King Bishnu Malla of Patan is said to have built a palace and placed a window having a golden image of Aryavalokiteshwara producing Brahma and other gods from his body (Wright, pp. 169-170).

Bishwabhu Buddha

In the Treta Yuga Bishwabhu Buddha of Anupam country had come to see the Swayambhu light residing on a mountain top which was named Pullochcha because he had offered one lakh of flowers to Swayambhu light. He also hinted to his disciples that the waters of Naga Hrada will be made to run out from certain places (Wright, pp. 50-51).

Bodhi Prakashan Kendra

In Patan a Bodhi Prakashan Kendra was founded on December 26, 1983 under the chairmanship of Dibya Bajra Bajracharya to publish Acharya Shanti Deva's work Bodhi Charyavatara. The centre has its president Satya Mohan Joshi, vice president Yajnaratna Dhakhwa, and treasurer Ananda Raj Shakya.

Brikha Deva, Buddhist King

In the genealogical work King Rudra Deva Varma's son Brikha Deva Varma is described to be very pious and he daily fed Bajra Jogini before taking his own meals. He is also described to have repaired the chaitya built by Dharma Datta, and built several Bihars for Bhikshus. We find a legend in the same source (Wright, p. 78) how Brikha Deva Varma returned from the hell and his founding of Pancha Buddha at Bandya gaon. It is said there that once when the king was visiting the Ashoka Stupa of

A Buddhist Painting (Pauwa) Lamaistic style.

Lagankhel he died there being attacked by severe illness. The servants of Yamaraja took him to their master's court. But Yamaraja chided his servants for having brought such a virtuous man to hell and was released and restored to life again. He then compared what he had seen in hell with what was written about it in the Karanda Byuha text and finding that they agreed, he became pleased. He built an image of Dharmaraja Lokeshvara and Yamantaka Agama. He also placed an image of Pancha Buddha at a village named Bandya gaon.

Buddha, the Lord

Buddha, the most enlightened one, is taken to have born at Lumbini in BC. 563 in the famous royal lineage of Shakya. King Shuddhodana was his father and Maya Devi was his mother, who had died only seven days after the Lord's birth. Hence the Lord was cared for by his mother's sister Maha Prajapati Gotami. In due course he was educated and married Yashodhara, daughter of the Kaliyan Suppa Buddha and sister of Devadatta. The couple had issued a son called Rahula.

But, Gautama Buddha left the palace secretly at night to become a hermit, when he was aged 29 only. Important events of his life are famous so we are not going to reproduce those here.

In Lord Buddha's personality we find most noble ideas relating to general public's life, his thinking and morals. But it is to be remembered here that Gautam Buddha based his essential theories on the Aryan ideals. He propagated his ideals in people's language, not in Sanskrit, the classical language used by other Rishis of earlier times. In another sense Buddha can be taken as a great Rishi of Aryan tradition, only he differed in his medium and democratic way. He had also borrowed democratic methods from the then republican states. This method of his concerned mainly the low caste people.

During the Lord's life-time the Sangha co-ordinated all his followers hence a type of religious organisation existed. But after the Lord's Mahaparinirvana Buddha's religion started its never-ending course of founding one sect or other not only in India but every where it reached and localized. But the innumerable sects related to Buddhism can well be taken as extension of the original religion.

The vast literature related to Buddhism and monuments found everywhere in Asia prove that mighty empire Buddhism has developed in the course of history. And, we Napalese can boast for that the Lord was born in Nepal.

Hundreds of scholars are needed to reveal the different aspects of Buddhism in modern language and mood.

Buddha Shakya Simha's Visit of Kathmandu Valley.

It is alleged in the genealogical work (Wright, pp. 73-74) that during Kirati King Jitedasti's time Shakya Simha Buddha came to the Valley from Kapilbastu and visited Swayambhu chaitya and Manjushri chaitya and fixed his abode at Pucchagra chaitya, west of Swayambhu Stupa. He is said to have accepted the worship and offerings of Chuda, a female Bhikshu, and made 1350 Proselytes, viz. Shaliputra, Mudgalyayana, Ananda etc. He is also described to have explained the glory of Swayambhu to Maitreya Bodhisattwa and others including Brahma who had come to see him.

Shakya Simha also visited Guhyeshwari and Namobuddha mountain to repair an old chaitya. Then he went to heaven to meet his mother who had died on the seventh day after his birth. Then, after preaching his doctrines to the people, he saw that the time of his death was approaching, and went to a city called Kusi. Here while he was preaching to an assembly of gods like Brahma and Bhikshus like Ananda, he disappeared. Some of his followers remained in Nepal and professed his religion.

In its succeeding parts, the genealogy mentions one Bhumi Varma who had been appointed successor by King Bhaskar Varma. This Bhumi Varma is said to have come here along with Shakya Simha Buddha and had settled here. He was of solar race of Rajputs and of Gautam Gotra, shared by Lord Buddha himself (Wright, p. 76). He was probably a Shakya.

Buddhism as the only Path of Salvation

A legend is contained in the genealogy that one ascetic, an incarnation of the famous Rishi Durbasa had commanded King Shiva Deva that in this age one cannot expect obtaining salvation without following Buddhism (Wright, p. 86).

Buddhist Priests of Pashupati

A brief reference contained in the genealogical work (Wright, pp. 81-82) suggests that before Shankaracharya's coming to the valley, Buddhist householder Brahmans acted as priests to Pashupati. But Shankaracharya had changed the rule and had appointed South Indian Brahmans as priests of Pashupati.

Buddhism vs Vaishnavism.

A legend contained in the genealogy suggests the feeling of Buddhism's superiority over Vaishnavism:

"A descendant of the Thakuris of Tiru Bahal, named Bhari - Bharo, being poor, used to store cakes of cow-dung (fuel) in his treasury, and revealed to no one what he had there. He used to carry the key with him where he went; but one day he forgot it, and his wife, finding it in his absence, opened the door, and saw that the room was full of ingots of gold. She told her husband, who was much surprised to find gold instead of cow-dung. Both of them, out of gratitude, became desirous to employ a portion of the gold for religious purposes. The wife, however, wished to do something for Narayana, and the husband for Buddha, and they could not agree which to prefer. At last they determined to sow the seed of Bhimpati and Tulsi, the former as an emblem of Buddha and the latter of Narayana; and whichever sprang up first was to decide which was to be the god of their worship. The Bhimpati came up first, so they followed the Buddhist religion. They invited Buddhists of the three cities on the 3rd of Phalgun, entertained them the whole night with feasting and an illumination of the house, and gave them leave to go away on the 4th. They then assigned lands for the maintenance of this custom, which is kept up to the present day" (Wright, p. 117.

Buddhist Migrants

In circa A.D. 1202 Bakhtkiyar Khilji had attacked upon Nadiya in Bengal. As a consequence of the attack, famed Buddhist scholars of Vikramashila University: Buddha Shri and Ratna Rakshita fled to Nepal accompanied by some followers. This event is recorded by Tibetan Lama and historian Taranath (Taranath, Shiefner, pp. 247, 253, 258, R.C. Mitra-Decline of Buddhism in India, Vishvabharati, 1954, p. 93).

Another wave of Buddhist immigrants had entered into Nepal in 1299 A.D. when Muslim attack on Bengal occured (V. Smith - History of Fine Art in India and Ceylon, 3rd ed. P. 202). These immigrants are considered responsible to bring the influences of Pala art in Nepal.

Buddhists vs Shaivites

A legend contained in the genealogy gives us the impression of Buddhist - Shaivite hatred and the superiority of Buddhism. The legend goes thus:

"The descendants of the Jhul Bahal Thakuris used to worship the Dasha Paramita Bauddha Devatas by washing their feet and feeding them in their houses with Khir (rice boiled in milk). To maintain this custom lands were set apart as trust. One of the descendants of these Thakuris had married a woman of Bhadgoan, and used to go to his father-in-law's house. One day, while conversing with his father-in-law, he told him that he worshipped Dasha Paramita Bauddha Devatas. The father-in-law said he would like to see them, and for this purpose went to Patan, and while his son-in-law was serving them with food, he mixed poison in something and laid it before them to eat. They, however, were aware of the treachery, and escaped the effect of the poison by repeating a Dharani or Buddhist verse. The Thakuri, who had given the poison, became affected by it, and no physician could cure him, but an astrologer told him that his disease was the work of some great deity. The son-in-law then entreated the Buddhist Devatas for his cure, and by their advice the water with which their feet had been washed was given to him to drink, and he was cured. From that day the deities came to be known, and the Thakuris worship ten old Bhikshus who represent them."

Buddhist-Shaivite Relations

Another legend contained in the genealogy refers to the hatred of Buddhists to Shankaracharya. According to the legend (Wright, pp. 107-8) out of hatred to Shankaracharya, a party of one thousand Bandas murdered seven hundred Brahmans residing in Bishalnagara. The wives of these Brahmans immolated themselves as Satis, and their curses were so powerful that the thousand murderers were burned to ashes. The spirits of these Satis then became so turbulent, that noone would venture to pass that way. The King Shankara Deva therefore, in order to put a stop to this trouble, caused an emblem of Shiva to be placed there by venerable pandits. This emblem, having been erected for the Shanti or peace, for the Brahma pishachas, was called Shanteshwara. It is also called Nandikeshwara from its having been erected by a Brahman of Bishalanagara, named Nandi, who himself after his death was deified as Mopta Deva or Bhat Bhatyani. After the seven hundred Brahmans had been massacred, the rest left Bishalnagara, and went to live at Deva Patan, where they built a house having seven courts.

Buddhists Associated with Pashuputi

One early King Bhaskara Varman is described, in one later type genealogy (Wright, pp. 75-76), to have conquered many countries upto Rameshwaram in South India through Pashupati's assistance. In his return he brought back much gold and dedicated those to Pashupati. He also caused Pashupati to be bathed with water containing gold, which ran down to the Bagmati river. The city of Dev Patan was also enlarged and named as Subarna Puri or golden town. The source further states that the king entrusted the daily worship, and the cremonies accompanying it to Buddhist householder Acharyas. The rules regarding the ceremonies of Pashupati were engraved on a copper plate which was given to the Bhikshus of Charumati Bihar to be kept in custody.

Chaitra Purnima

Bipashwi Buddha had sowed a lotus seed in the Naga Hrad on the Chaitra Purnima day having his abode at Jat Matrocha or Nagarjun mountain. The occasion is now commemorated going for pilgrimage to the Nagarjun mountain.

Chaitya of Devapatan

One King Shiva Deva is described in the genealogy to have unearthed a Chaitya which was concealed by Shankaracharya in Deopatan (Wright, p. 84).

Chaitya at Minanatha

In A.D. 1673 one Satyaram Bharo of Tangal Tol repaired the chaitya and the bathing place in front of Minanatha (Wright, p. 167).

Chaitya at Parsa

Some have found the remains of a Buddhist Chaitya in Parsa district in Murali Panchayat, east of Birganj. The remains are scattered around 2 bighas of land. One Bhikshu Vagindra Vajra has constituted a committee to renovate the Chaitya which is taken similar to that of so-called Ashokan Stupas of Patan (Gorkha Patra, Vaishakh 11, 2037).

Chakra Maha Bihar

King Mana Deva is said to have built the Chakra Bihar near the Matirajya Ashoka Stupa which was known as Mana Deva Samskarita Chakra Maha Bihar (Wright, p. 83).

Charumati

The genealogical work (Wright, pp. 74-75) contains a legend relating King Ashoka's visit of the valley along with his daughter Charumati. The Princess Charumati, while playing one day, saw an iron arrowhead turned into stone by a god, and determined to remain in Nepal, having concluded from this that it was a land of miracles wrought by the gods. Therefore, Ashoka gave her in marriage to a Kshatriya Devapala, and gave them 3600 ropanis of land and other requirements for their maintenance. The couple then founded and peopled Deva Pattan. After rearing a large family and becoming aged they wished to live in retirement in a Bihara. A Bihara was built and was named after the Princess Charumati where she died as a Bhikshuni. But Devapala could not build a Bihara of his own hence he died in great distress.

Charumati Bihara

Ashoka's daughter Charumati is said in the genealogical work to have built a Bihar in Deva Pattan where she had died in her old age as a Bhikshuni (Wright, pp. 74-75).

King Bhaskar Varman is described in the genealogy to have enlarged the Deva Pattan and naming it as Suvarna Puri or golden town and caused the Pashupati to be bathed with water containing gold. But the king entrusted the daily worship, and the ceremonies accompanying it, to Buddhist householder Acharyas. The rules and ceremonies to be observed were engraved on a copper plate and lodged at the Charumati Bihar (Wright, p. 76). The Suvarna Puri itself was dedicated to Lord Pashupati by the king.

Later Shankaracharya had replaced the rules engraved on the copper plate and a new rule for sacrificing animals had been added there (Wright, p. 82).

The Bihara is also called Chavahil Bihara or Suvarna Pura Kirtipunya Ashoka Samskarita Mahavihara.

Chiniya Lama

According to Colonel Santabir Lama the Chinese Government had appointed a Chinese Lama to protect the Stupa of Bauddha. The Lama's descendants are now called Chiniya Lama who are responsible to upkeep the Stupa and its property *(Nangba Sange, p. 87)*. Some ppeople take him as Dalai Lama's representative.

The elder Chiniya Lama died on July 18, 1982

at the age of 93. His real name was Punya Bajra Lama, son of Buddha Bajra Lama. He also swayed over the Melamchi Gumba in Helambu.

Classification of Biharas

The Buddhist Newars classify the Viharas into the following three types:

1. ***Kacha Baha:*** Buddhist families reside in such Vihars. It is also called as `Kacha Baha' or Branch Montery (Ratna Jyoti Shakya, op. cit. p. 16). Initiation ritual is not done here.

2. ***Bahi Vihar:*** `Only lay scholars lived in such Vihars which are mainly used as the centre of academic and religious activities (Ratna Jyoti, ibid.). Initiation ritual can be done here.

3. ***Maha Viharas:*** Only celibate monks can live in such Viharas and practice sectarian rites. Initiation or ordaining ceremony can be done here.

Dasha Paramita Bauddha Devatas

To worship the deity any ten old men from any Bihar are taken and worshipped as gods. Their feet, are washed and they are fed as prescribed. The names of the original Devatas are:

1. Dana Paramita
2. Shila Paramita
3. Kshanti Paramita
4. Birya Paramita
5. Dhyana Paramita
6. Prania Paramita
7. Upaya Paramita

8. Bala Paramita
9. Pranidhi Paramita
10. Gyana Paramita

Deity of Pingala Bahal

During King Bhaskara Deva's reign the Bandas of Pingala Bahal are said to have removed to other places. Their descendants who were Acharyas became Bandas and lived in Gnakha Chok in Patan (near the western gate of Patan). The Bhikshus of Devapatan and Chabahil came to these people and told them that they had heard from some people, who were working in the fields, that they had seen the god of Pingala Bahal. They accordingly went to see, and found the god buried under the ruins of the Pingala Bahal, and brought him to Patan, while they were taking him thither, when they had arrived at a bow shot north of Mangal Bhatta, they saw Lakshmi Devi of Lagankhel in the form of a kite, and one of the devotees, by the influence of his Mantras, brought her down, and the Devi became stationery there in the road. After this, they took the god Gnakhachok, but he said he would not like to live there. This having been brought to the notice of King Bhaskara Deva, he caused a new Bihar, named Nhul Bahal, to be built for the god. This new house also being disapproved of by the god, the king went to ask where he would like to fix his residence. Then the king built Hema Barma Bihar (Wright, p. 106).

Dharma Datta Chaitya

One King Brikhadeva Varma is said to have repaired the chaitya built by Dharma Datta (Wright, p. 78).

King Dharma Deva is also recorded in the genealogy to have repaired the Dhanado chaitya built by King Dharma Datta (Wright, p. 83).

Dharmakara, First King

Manjushri Bodhisattwa is said in the genealogical work to have appointed the first King Dharmakara in the Manju Pattan city. He is described to be issueless hence he had appointed his successor one Dharma Pal who had come with Krakucchanda Buddha (Wright, p. 54).

Dharmalabha Buddhist Festival

On the day of Gaijatra (Late August) (Bhadra Krishna Pratipada) Buddhists in Patan worship at the four so called Ashokan stupas: Namely - Ibahil, Treta, Lagankhel and Pulchok after bathing in the Bagmati river at Shankhamul Ghat. Buddhists also donate fruits on this occasion. The deity Jatadhari Lokeshwara of Jyesthavarna Maha Bihar is also particularly worshipped. On this occasion people also bathe in the Prayag Pokhari, a sacred pond.

Dharama Pal King

The first king of Manju Pattan city Dharamakar was issueless; he had appointed his successor one Dharmapal who had come with Krakucchanda Buddha (Wright, p. 54).

Dharmashri Mitra

In the genealogical work a legend related to the Bikramshil Bihar of Thamel and the contact between Manjushri and Dharmashri Mitra of Vikram Shila Bihar of Benares (?) (Wright, p. 55):

Once Dharmashri Mitra, a Pandit of Bikramashil Vihar of Benares was reciting some moral traditions from a scripture, when he came to the secret Mantra of 12 letters which he could not explain. To get the Mantra explained from Manjushri he came to Swayambhu. Manjushri knew the Pandit's intention and came to Nepal and began to plough a field having yoked for that purpose a lion and a Shardul (griffin). Seeing this strange sight Dharmshri Mitra went up to Manjushri and asked the way to China. Manjushri replied that, it was too late to commence his journey, and took him to his house, where he instantly caused a good Bihar to spring up, in which he lodged his guest. During the night Dharmashri Mitra overheard some conversation between Manjushri and his wife, which made known to him the disguised Manjushri and he slept at the threshold of his room. In the morning Manjushri made him his disciple and told him the meaning of the Mantra. The Bihar in which he had lodged he called Bikramashil Bihar and the field which he was ploughing when met by Dharmashri Mitra, he called Sawa Bhumi; and to this day this is the field in which rice is planted before all the other fields in the valley. The field belongs to the priest of the Bihar.

Dharmodaya Sabha

The exiled Nepalese Buddhist Bhikshus meet at Sarnath (India) on November 30, 1944 to found the Dharmodaya Sabha to serve the Nepalese Buddhists. Venerable U. Chandramani Mahasthavir and Bhadanta Ananda Kaushalyayana were elected president and vice president respectively of the newly formed Buddhist committee. The Sabha had two main objects: to propagate the true teachings of Buddha by publications and to encourage Buddhist studies. Afterwards the Sabha contributed much to the Newari Buddhist literature to prosper.

In 1946 venerable Narda Mahathera led a goodwill mission from Ceylon to Nepal. The mission became able to get permission from the Nepal Government to build a chaitya in Kathmandu which was named after Ceylon. Afterwards ven. Narada Mahathera came again in Kathmandu to inaugurate the chaitya where a sacred relic brought from Ceylon was enshrined. The monk had also brought a sapling of the sacred Bo tree of Anuradhapura which was planted here. The then Prime Minister Mohan Shamsher accepted ven. Narada Mahathera's suggestion that the Buddhist Government officials be given a holiday on the thrice-sacred day of Vaishakh Purnima.

After 1950 the Sabha offices had shifted to Kathmandu and continues to publish its journal Dharmodaya. The Sabha has also established many Viharas in Patan, Kathmandu, Bhojpur, Pokhara and Tansen. The Sabha also brought Nepal the sacred relics of Sariputta and Mahamoggallyayana from India. A Buddhist residential school Anandakuti Vidyapitha was also established by the Sabha.

The Sabha has also been participating in international Buddhist conferences. Bhikshu Amritananda and Shri Maniharsha Jyoti represented the Sabha to the First World Buddhist Conference held in Ceylon. Bhikshu Amritananda and Keshar Lal had represented the Sabha to the Second World Buddhist Conference held in Japan.

Dharmodaya Sabha is a Theravadin Buddhist Organisation which has reintroduced the original Theravadin Buddhism in Nepal.

Dhyanochcha Mountain

The mountain top from which Shikhi Buddha from Arun Puri, had meditated on the Swayambhu light was called Dhyanochcha (Wright, p. 50). This name is identified with the mount now called as Champa Devi east of Chandagiri mountain near Thankot in the southern part of the valley. It is also called Dhyanacho.

Dipa Yatra Festival, Patan

On the Bhadra Krishna Dwitiya (Tritiya ?) day (August 25, 1983: Bhadra 9, 2040) the Buddhists of Patan observe the 'Mata-Ya' or Dipa Yatra festival. On this occasion the Buddhists of Patan go round the city of Patan starting from Saugal tol and pay homage to all the Buddhist shrines (said to be 2500) within the city of Patan. It is believed that one Lichchavi King Balarchana Deva had initiated this festival about 12 hundred years ago.

Dullu, Buddhism in

In far western Nepal in Dullu is found a stone column having an inscription of Khasa Malla King Ashoka Challa's time (ca. 13th century ?). The upper part of the column bears a carving of Buddha. The undated inscription (Gorkha Patra, VS. 2033 Vaishakh, 26, quoted by Suryamani Adhikari, op. cit.) starts with salutations to Lord Buddha. According to the inscription the temple (Devala) was built by Sauna Karki and his wife Sauka Karkyani.

Four Buddhas of Devapatan

One King Shiva Deva is described in the genealogy to have established four Buddhas in the city of Navatol near Deopatan when he had founded the city and installed many other gods to protect it (Wright, p. 84).

Gandheshvara Vaitaraga

Gandheshvara is taken by Buddhists as one of the eight vaitaragas (Wright, p. 59).

In another instance a genealogical work states that Gandheshvara was originated from Kshiti Garbha Bodhisattwa who had left his spirit in the umbrella established by Odiya Acharya who was engaged in a grand ritual (Wright, p. 68).

Ganesha of the Buddhists

The Ganesha image seen at the Mhaipi shrine has been identified by Dhana Shamsher Rana as the Ganesha of the Buddhists (Kamakalarahasya, p. 102).

Godabari

During King Bikramajit's time goddess Basundhara Devi of Phullochcha mountain is stated in the genealogy to have discovered Godabari on the Simha Sankranti (the day when the sun enters Leo), and at that time the Planet Guru (Jupiter) was also in Leo. Because Basundhara discovered Godabari, any one who digs a well or builds a dhara or hiti, first worship her (Wright, p. 65).

Gorakhnath

In one type of genealogy Gorakhnath had attracted the nine Nagas into a hillock and sat down upon it to cause a drought for 12 years in Nepal during King Bara Deva's reign. He had done all this because he wanted to see Matsyendranatha, who was the Lokeshwara or the Lord of the universe (Wright, pp. 93-102).

Guhyeshwari Bishwarupa

In genealogical work Manjushri Bodhisattwa is said to have discovered Guhyeshwari in the form of Bishwarupa on the Paush Krishna 9th day after he had seen Bishwarupa Swayambhu. The root of the lotus flower which contained the Swayambhu light is also stated to have its origin in Guhyeshwari (Wright, p. 51).

Krakucchanda Buddha is also said in the same genealogical work to have seen Guhyeshwari in the form of the Swayambhu light and had preached the significance of the gooddess (Wright, p. 52).

In the same genealogical work we find Shakya Simha Buddha also described to have visited the Guhyeshwari shrine (Wright, p. 73).

Gunakama Deva, King

In Swayambhu Purana a great drought is described during one King Gunakama Deva's reign. Some have taken him who ruled Nepal during 942-1008 A.D. In one MSS colophon dated A.D. 1045 we find King Gunakama Deva to have built a Buddhist Vihara named Padmachakra Mahavihara *(Medieval Nepal, I. p. 123).*

Various kings named Gunakama Deva are found recorded in various sources of Nepalese history since ancient period to medieval times. Various miraculous legends are also recorded in genealogies describing the king doing numerous acts of virtues related to Shaivism or Buddhism. Afterwards we will try to ascertain the different Gunakama Devas and their contributions.

Gunakirti Mahavihar, Thimi

At Digutol, Thimi Gunakirti Mahavihar is famous. The copper plate inscription dated NS. 696 of King Sadashiva Malla's time which was attached to the Vihar mentions name of the Vihar as Gunakirti Heravarna Mahavihar.

Gunla Dharma or Bauddha Yatra

Newar Buddhists observe a month long festival during Shravan Shukla Pratipada to Bhadra Krishna Amavasya.

According to one source *(Devamala Vamshavali, p. 102)* the custom was started by King Vikrama Sena in Kaliguata year 2973 as counselled by one Maheshvāra Thakur.

Gyana Dakini

In the genealogical work we find the goddess as the mother of Aryavalokiteshwara Matsyendra Natha.

Halahala Lokeswara

The Newar Buddhists take the Nilakantha of Gosainkunda as Halahala Lokeshvara and go there for pilgrimage to offer prayers.

Hari-Hari Bahana Lokeshwara

In the genealogical work (Wright, pp. 62-63) we find the following legend regarding the event of

Lokeshvara's calling as Hari-Hari Bahan Lokeshwara:

> After Lokeshvara made Kulika Naga immovable mountain, another celebrated Naga, who was also formerly completed by Manjushri to leave the valley, became angry, when it was again under water, and began to bite people without any provocation. This sin produced leprosy in his body, and, to expiate his offence against Manjushri, he returned to Nepal, and began to practice austerities at Gokarna, when the prince Gokarna had obtained salvation. Garuda, the vehicle of Lord Vishnu, seeing him, came to catch him, but he being more powerful than the former, on account of the austerities he had practised, caught hold of Garuda, and kept his head under water. Garuda then invoked the aid of his master Vishnu, who came, and was going to strike Takshaka Naga with his Chakra (discus); but in the meantime Aryavalokiteshvara Padmapani Bodhisattwa, seeing that a Naga observing austerities, was being killed, came from Sukhavati Bhuvan (heaven) to protect him. Vishnu then took him on his shoulders, and the Lokeshwara caused friendship to be established between Garuda and Takshaka, and put the latter round Garuda's neck.
>
> Then Garuda lifted up Vishnu, and the lion, which had been ridden by the Lokeshwara, lifted up Garuda, and, flying up into the air, alighted on a mountain, which was named Hari-Hari Bahan or Changu, where the Lokeshwara disappeared. This mountain was in consequence named Charu, but since then it has been

corrupted into Changu.

The legend thus suggests that the Buddhists identify Changu Narayana with Buddhist deity Bodhisattwa Avalokiteshwara.

We have such an image installed at the courtyard of the Swayambhu Stupa. In the north of the said Stupa the stone sculpture of Hari-Hari Vahana Lokeshwara is attached to the western side of a platform. The image is about 3 feet in height which depicts a six handed Lokeshvara sitting over four handed Narayana who again is seated upon Garuda, the latter crouching over a lion. Three small size human figures appear in both sides of the central figure. This sculpture is undated but can be assigned to the 18th century period or late Malla period.

Hariti

In the Swayambhu Purana we find reference to the Goddess Hariti which has been said to be a Yakshini. She is described there having issued 500sons. The Purana also states that those Shaivites who also worship Buddha do worship the Goddess Hariti (H.P. Shastri, Swayambhu Purana, p. 428). There is a shrine at the temple of Maiti Devi, who is called Dhana Bhaju, a son of goddess Hariti.

Hatko Bihar

Patan King Siddhi Narasimha Malla is said in the genealogical work to have caused to be pulled down Hatko Bihar and rebuilt near Gau Bahal because the Bihar was built near the Mulchok of the royal palace (Wright, p. 159). The Bihar is said to have been built by one Lakshmikama Deva Barma.

Hema Barna Bihara

When Nuwakot Thakuri King Bhaskara Deva wanted to build a Bihar for the deity of Pingala Bihar in Patan he first built Nhul Bahal. But the deity disapproved this Bihar, and the king asked the deity where he would like to fix his residence. The god said he would like to live in a place where a mouse attacked and drove away a cat. The king himself then went in search of such a place and one day at a certain place saw a golden mouse chasing a cat. On that spot the king built a Bihar and named it Hema Barna or golden coloured and having placed the god in it, with Agama Devatas just as they were in Pingala Bahal, he assigned lands for its maintenance. The Bandas, who came with the god to reside here, were those of Thya Kayel and Hatakha tol (Wright, p. 106).

Imado Chaitya

In the genealogical work we find reference to the origin of one of the four so called Ashokan Stupas of Patan. This legend (Wright, p. 69) relates to the eastern Stupa which is called Imado chaitya. According to the said source there was a chaitya in Bishal Nagara (Kathmandu) which was not destroyed by the flood caused by Danasur. Its votaries, not being able to support themselves when Bishal Nagara was destroyed, thought of removing. One night they were told in a vision that they were to remove to a place which would be indicated by a bird flying from the chaitya. In the morning they saw a kite perched on the top of the chaitya which on their approach flew away, and alighted again at a spot where they raised another chaitya, and named it Imado, from Ima, or a kite. The chaitya is half a mile to the east of the

Patan city.

Itam Bahal

A legend contained in the genealogy gives the origin of the Itam Bahal. According to the legend (Wright, pp. 113-115) a Thakuri, named Bhaskara Malla lived in the city of Kathmandu. He had a son named Keshachandra. He was a minor, when his father died, and unable to take care of his own affairs. So his father appointed a guardian.

Keshachandra, however, being of a truant disposition, used to give his guardian the slip and go gambling here and there. One day he went to Tham Bahil, where he saw the deity being repaired by the descendants of Simhal. This deity was erected by Simhal, but was destroyed when Danasur flooded the valley. He began gambling there, and as it was late, instead of returning home, he went to the house of his sister, who lived at Tam Bahil. His sister reproved him for playing so late an hour, but he paid no attention to her, and after taking his meal, he again went out to gamble. He lost heavily, and returned to the house of his sister, who again reproved him, but with so little effect that Keshachandra now took away and staked the plate on which he had eaten his meal, and lost it. When he returned he found that his food was served on the ground, which so affronted him that he tied up the rice in his clothes and going home he put it in a corner. To relieve his mind from the feeling of degradation he went to Nilakantha Gosain Than and having bathed in the lake, prayed to the deity, and asked for help Nilakantha's voice replied from the sky, that he should visit Pashupati and Kirthimukha Bhairava, and his misery should be ended.Keshachandra did as he was directed, and seeing that the offering of rice before Kirtimukha was so rotten that the grain had become full of maggots, he gathered it up, and took it home. His curiosity then led him to go and see in what condition the rice was which he had brought from his sister's house. This also was rotten, and Keshachandra not knowing what to do with it, begged for and obtained a quantity of rice from some other people, and mixing the rotton rice with this, he went to sell it. He exchanged it for some Marcha (the refused rice that remains after distilling spirit), and went to a place named Bakhuncha, where he spread it out to dry, as it was wet, and then went to sleep. While he slept pigeons came and ate the marcha, and being told by Kirtimukha Bhairava to give something in return, they left golden dung on the spot. Keshachandra, having awoke, was gathering the gold, when a Rakshasha named Gurung Mapa, came by, and was about to devour him; but being addressed as Mama (maternal uncle) the Rakshasa was appeared and helped Keshachandra to carry the gold to his home. Keshachandra then married the daughter of King Hari Deva.

Keshachandra kept the Rakshasa in his house, and told him that he might have the bodies of all the persons who died there for his food. This gave much annoyance to the people, and caused a great deal of misery, for when parents said to frighten their crying children into silence. The Rakshasa (demon) took them at their word, and soon devoured them. The people therefore complained to Keshachandra. He bought 360 ropanis of land, which he had levelled into a plain ground, and called it Tundikhel, because he had purchased the land with gold begotton by tudi, or maggots, produced in rotton grain. Hen then gave this ground to Gurung Mapa as his residence, on condition that he was not to devour any one, and was never for his service Keshachandra promised to send him every year a muri of rice and a buffalo for his food.

Keshachandra's son having died in his youth, he took his body to burn, and having ascended into the sky by means of the smoke, he saw his son above him in the clouds mounting upwards. Having come down again, he performed the funeral rites. He then returned home and built a Bihar, in which he placed a Buddha and assigned a Guthi (trust) for feeding pigeons with 102 *aris* of unhusked rice because all his wealth was derived from pigeons. The Bihar he named Parabata Bihar from Parabata, a pigeon. He also assigned a Guthi (trust) to place on the Tundikhel one *aris* of boiled rice, and one cauldron full of flesh, for Gurung Mapa on the anniversary of the 14th of Phaigun Badi. Keshachandra, then caused a picture of all these circumstances to be made, and put it in his Bihar, where he lived as a devotee of Buddha. This picture is shown to those who wish to see it in the month of Shrawan. People afterwards named this Bihar Itam Bahal.

In Gopala Vamshavali we find 'Yatumbahara Kwatha for A.D. 1241 (GV. p. 33B). This refers that Itam Bahal was built as a fort to protect its riches. (Gautam Bajra - Hanuman Dhoka, p. 38).

Jamana Gubhaju

One Gu Bahal (or Buddhist Guru) by name Jamana, is recorded in the genealogical work, as the advisor to the repairing works of the Itam Bahal, built by Keshachandra. The Gubhaju is also described there to have taught many arts to King Pratapa Malla (Wright, p. 150).

Jatadhari Lokeshvara

There is a temple of Jatadhari Lokeshvara at Tangal Tol in Patan which is believed to have been built by King Amshu Varman.

Jata Matrocha

Bipashwi Buddha had lived on a mountain top which he later named as Jata Matrocha, now called as Nagarjun hill.

Jayasthiti Malla and Buddhism

King Jayasthiti Malla is mentioned in the genealogy to have caused to have erected in various places the Agama Devatas of the Buddhists (Wright, p. 124).

Kanaka Chaitya

Kanaka Muni Buddha is stated in the genealogy to have visited Swayambhu and Guhyeshwari in Dwapara Yuga (Wright, p. 54). He is also said to have ascended into heaven and to have caused Lord Indra to practise virtue (see Niglihawa).

Kankre Bihar Surkhet

In Surkhet valley in south-western inner tarai huge remains of Buddhist monuments are seen. This site is locally called as Kankre Bihar.

According to reports the remains are scattered within a 350 circuit area on a mound having 20 feet elevation. Here besides the stone images of Padmapani Bodhisattwa, Avalokiteshvara and goddess Tara Hindu gods are found lying (Suryamani Adhikari - Kakrevihardekhi Rarasamma Madhuparka, Vol. 12, No. 4, August - September 1979, pp. 95-105).

Kapotala

The place where Matsyendra Nath was incarnated. The place is in Assam.

Karkotaka

Karkotaka is described in the genealogical work as the King of Nagas living in the great lake covering the Kathmandu Valley. When Manjushri Bodhisattwa had cut through the hills to let the water run out the Naga King wanted to escape outside but Manjushri had persuaded him to remain here in the Taudaha lake having an authority over the wealth of the valley (Wright, p. 51).

Kartik Purnima.

The day when Manjushri Bodhisattwa got the vision of Swayambhu as Bishwarupa in the middle of the lotus flower whose root was at Guhyeshwari, as recorded in the genealogical work (Wright, p. 51).

Kashyapa Buddha

In Dwapara Yuga after Kanaka Muni Buddha's visit Kashyapa Buddha of Benares is also stated in the genealogy to have come to visit the Swayambhu and Guhyeshwari shrines (Wright, p. 54). From here he went to Gauda country (Bengal) where the King Prachanda Deva offered him a Pindapatra (sacrificial vessel). Kashyapa Buddha suggested to the king to go to Swayambhu and became a disciple of Gunakara Bhikshu a follower of Manjushri. Kashyapa then returned to his own country.

Kathmandu Viharas

There are thirty important Buddhist Viharas in Kathmandu (Hemaraj Shakya Bhaskarakirti Mahavihar, p. 55 table). Among these vihars the following sixteen are of Bahi types:

1. *Shri Jotikirti Mahavihara*
   or Syangu Bahi (Swayambhu)
2. *Shri Kirtana Mahavihar*
   or Kinu Bahi (Kimdol)
3. *Shri Vidyeshvari Mahavihara*
   or Vilasa Bahi (Bijayeshvari)
4. *Shri Nadisangama Mahavihara*
   or Khusi Bahi (Tahachal)
5. *Shri Bikramashila Mahavihara*
   or Tham Bahi (Thamel)
6. *Shri Gaganasangama Mahavihara*
   or Gana Bahi (Gana Bahal)
7. *Shri Shadakshari Mahavihara*
   or Dugam Bahi (New Road)
8. *Shri Rajakirti Mahavihara*
   or Makhan Bahi (Makhan Tol)
9. *Shri Pradyotakirti Mahavihara*
   or Nah Bahi (Jorganesh)
10. *Shri Kirtipunya Mahavihara*
    or Nhayakam Bahi (Lagan)

Sunayashri Mishra Stupa at Patan.

11. *Shri Kirtipunya Mahavihara*
    or Chvakam Bahi (Lagan)
12. *Shri Shakyaketu Mahavihara*
    or Maru Bahi (Lagan)
13. *Shri Italamkhu Paravarta Mahavihara*
    or Arakhu Bahi (Yetkha)
14. *Shri Italamkhu Mahavihara*
    or Mahaka Bahi (Yetkha)
15. *Shri Muktipur Mahavihara*
    or Mukun Bahi (Damai Tol)
16. *Shri Naka Mahavihara*
    or Layaku Bahi (Hanuman Dhoka)

The following eighteen are Mu Baha of Kathmandu:

1. *Shri Maitripura Mahavihara*
   or Kwa Baha (Thanhiti)
2. *Shri Karunapura Mahavihara*
   or Cchusya Baha (Jyatha Tol)
3. *Shri Hemakara Mahavihara*
   or Dhoka Baha (Tyaud)
4. *Shri Hemavarna Mahavihara*
   or Gam Baha (Tyaud)
5. *Shri Ratnaketu Mahavihara*
   or Nhu Baha (Thayamadu or Bangemudha)
6. *Shri Suratashri Mahavihara*
   or Tacche Baha (Asan)
7. *Shri Rajakriti Mahavihara*
   or Te Baha (Te Bahal)

8. *Shri Paravata Mahavihara*
or Itum Baha (Itam Bahal)
9. *Shri Kanaka Chaitya Mahavihara*
or Jan Baha (Kel Tol)
10. *Shri Mulashri Mahavihara*
or Mu Baha (Watu Tol)
11. *Shri Mantrasiddhi Mahavihara*
or Saval Baha (Watu Tol)
12. *Shri Mantrasiddhi Mahavihara*
or Saval Baha (Watu Tol)
13. *Shri Tarumul Mahavihara*
or Sikhonmu Baha (Maru Tol)
14. *Shri Brahmachakra Mahavihara*
or Om Baha (Jorganesh)
15. *Shri Ratnakirti Mahavihara*
or Makhan Baha (Makhan Tol)
16. *Shri Vajrashila Mahavihara*
or Iku Baha (Yangal)
17. *Shri Kirtipunya Mahavihara*
or Lagan Baha (Lagan Tol)
18. *Shri Manisangha Mahavihara*
or Musum Baha (Brahma Tol)

Keshabati or Bishnumati River

The genealogical work states that in Treta Yuga Krakucchanda Buddha had visited the valley for his many auspicious activities (Wright, p. 52). When once he started to ordain 700 disciples into monkhood half the hair shaved from his disciples was buried in a mound on the mountain and other half he threw up into the air. Wherever the hair fell a stream was formed which was called Keshavati because it was formed by Kesha or hair. In memory of the auspicious event people go to the mountain to bathe in the river, because of its sanctity in having brought forth by Krakucchanda Buddha's command. On that occasion people visit the Kesha chaitya also.

Kesha Chaitya

When Krakucchanda Buddha buried half the hair shaved from his disciple's heads under a mound (chaitya) on the Shivapuri mountain it was called as Kesha chaitya as alleged in the genealogical work (Wright, p. 52).

Khasarpa Lokeshwara

King Gunakama Deva in imitation of the Lokeshwara Jatra of Patan, he made an image of Khasarpa Lokeshwara, and caused his Jatra to be celebrated annually (Wright, p. 104).

Kotwal

As the genealogical work states that the Manjushri Bodhisattwa had cut the mountain to let the valley water run out and the place of cutting was named as Kotwal (or Kotwal dwar) (Wright, p. 51). As the event had occurred on the Baishakh Sankranti Day the day is commemorated by bathing in Bagmati in Chobhar.

Krakucchanda Buddha

As the genealogical work relates (Wright, p. 52-53) after Manjushri's feats in Treta Yuga Krakucchanda Buddha came from Kshemavati and saw Guhyeshwari in the form of the Swayambhu light, which led him to think of consecrating a mountain, after the example of the other former Buddhas, who had formerly visited the place. With such intention he ascended the high mountain to the north and lived there. He then explained the merits of Swayambhu and Guhyeshwari to his followers and instructed them in the ways and doctrines of Grihasthas (householders) and Bhikshus (mendicants). Then he permitted seven hundred of his disciples, including one Brahmin Abhayananda and one Kshatriya Gunadhwaja to live as Bhikshus. But finding no water on the mountain with which to perform the sprinkling on them he called on Swayambhu and Guhyeshwari and said "Let water run out of this mountain". At the same time he thrust his thumb into the mountain and made a hole through which Ganga Devi appeared in corporal form and offered water to Buddha, and then changing her form into water, ran out of the mountain on the Mesha Sankranti Day (Vaishakh Sankranti day), and became known as Bagmati. With this water Krakucchanda Buddha then performed sprinkling and anointation. Half of the hair cut from his disciple's heads on the mountain he buried under a mound, and the other half he threw up into the air. Wherever the hair fell, a stream was formed, which was called Keshavati, from Kesha or hair. Hence, on the Mesha Sankranti day, people go to this mountain to bathe in the river, because of its sanctity in having been brought forth by the command of Krakucchanda, whence also the place was named Bagdwar. People also visit the Kesha chaitya, and bathe at the source of the Keshavati river on the same day.

After doing all this Krakucchanda Buddha

preached the four castes of the peoples the way of living as householders and Bhikshus worshipping Swayambhu and Guhyeshwari, and saw in the wood planted by Manjushri the three gods: Brahma, Vishnu and Maheshvara in the form of deer. He also pointed out these to his disciples as worshippers of Swayambhu and Guhyeshwari and protectors of the people. He also said that they had come there as prophesied by Padmapani Bodhisattwa Lokeshwara to whom they had given their promise to that effect and had foretold that in Kali Yuga Umeshwar Pashupati would be a very celebrated name. He then called the place Mrigasthali after the three deities who appeared there in the form of deer. He then permitted those of his disciples who wished to live as householders to inhabit in Manju Pattan city, and to those who wished to live as Bhikshus he allotted Viharas and temples and returned to his former abode.

Kulika Naga Changed into Kileshwara Mountain

It is said in the genealogical work (Wright, p. 62) that Kulika Naga had gone out of the lake when Manjushri had dried up the lake of the valley. Later when Danasur made a lake again Kulika Naga had returned to live here. Aryavalokiteshwara Padmapani Bodhisattwa, seeing that this Kulika Naga was spoiling the memorial of Manjushri, sent Samanta Bhadra Bodhisattwa to make him immovable. He went and sat on the Naga's back and became a mountain, called Kileshwara (Changu), on which he left a portion of his spirit and then disappeared.

Kumari Cult

About Kumari cult we find a reference in the genealogy that King Gunakama Deva's grand son Lakshmikama Deva thinking that his grand father had acquired so much wealth and conquered the four quarters of the world through the aid of the Kumaris, resolved to do the same. To do this he went to Patan Darbar and having worshipped as Kumari the daughter of a Bandya (Banda), living in a Bihar near the palace known as Lakshmi Barman, he erected an image of Kumari and established the Kumari Puja (Wright, p. 105).

The last Malla King of Kathmandu had introduced the Kumari cult in a new fashion. While the king himself was a Shaivite but he seems to have incorporated many Buddhist elements in this cult. The origin of the Kumari worship in King Jayaprakasha Malla's time is also related to Buddhist persons. We quote here the legend relating to the origin of the cult in King Jayaprakasha Malla's time:

One day a Jyapu person became haunted by a god and he started trembling and squatting on the stone emblem of Pancha Linga Bhairava (Pachali). Seeing this people asked him his name. Being asked such the Jyapu asked the people to bring King Jayaprakasha Malla to find the answer. Messengers rushed to the royal palace to report the mystic message. Since the king was destined to be deprived of his Kingdom he became angry and said - the Jyapu is drunk in the feast and does not acknowledge even the king, so I would not leave him free. Then he brought the Jyapu in the royal palace and asked him. But the Jyapu kept quiet and began trembling. He was molested and was bound by rope to the elephant post consequently he died. Next day the Jyapu's

property was forfeited.

Then afterwards another Jyapu became haunted again. King Jayaprakasha having heard this went to ask him. The Jyapu did not face the king and replied - you have molested and humiliated the first Jyapu I had haunted. You will lose your Kingdom. Hearing this curse the king tried to pacify the goddess but failed and returned to the palace. The same night Kumari Devi granted vision to the king in his dream. She said angrily - Oh Jayaprakasha Malla ! I had haunted that person to grant you boon but you made me humiliated and killed him thoughtlessly. Hereafter do not bear love for the Kingdom since it is to be occupied by the enemy.

Dreaming that King Jayaprakasha Malla became worried. But he thought to please and pacify the goddess by honouring her. Again he constituted a Jatra to please the goddess. He built a house according to the prescribed rules of Bastu Chakra. He also built a beautiful chariot having an appearance of the mystic diagram (Yantra) and instituted Kumari Jatra during Indrajatra days accompanied by Ganesha and Batuka (a form of Bhairava) (Bhasha Vamshavali, Pt. 2. Editor Devi Prasad Lamsal, Nepal Rashtriya Pustakalaya, VS. 2023, pp. 117-118).

We have another version of the event (Yogi Naraharinatha - *Devamala Vamshavali.* pp.77-78) which does not refer to the Jyapu's being haunted. But it states that the Goddess Kumari became angry with Jayaprakasha Malla and said that the king will loose his Kingdom. When the king promised to the virgin goddess of special worship and a chariot drawing festival, the goddess granted 12 years more ruling period.

A Thyasaphu (dairy) note has recorded the event (Gautam Bajra Vajracharya - Hanumandhoka Raja Darbar, pp. 42-43). According to the diary King Jayaprakasha Malla had built the house for Kumari in 7 months of A.D. 1757. The ritual was performed through the Vajracharyas who had also read a Buddhist text of Panchavimshatika. On the occasion Pashupati, Swayambhu and many other deities were invited. All Kanphatta Nath Yogis were invited to be fed.

Kumari worshipped in Hanumandhoka is believed to be the mortal form of Tulaja Devi the patron deity of the Malla Kings.

Kwa Bahal Bauddha Temple Patan

In one genealogical work *(Devamala Vamshavali, p. 71)* it is alleged that the Kwa Bahal Bauddha temple was built by one Brahman of Mithila country who had gone to Lhasa in Tibet. When he returned to his country after earning riches he became an outcast by his relatives and hence he came to Nepal and converted into Buddhism. Here in Kaligata year 3610-11 (A.D. 508-9) during King Bira Deva's reign he built a Buddhist image and a Vihara to reside and later died here. In the great earthquake of 1934 the Vihar remained intact.

Lagan Bahal

According to the genealogical work (Wright, p. 148) during King Pratap Malla's reign one Sumaraj Shakya Bhikshu built the Lagan Bahal in the Kathmandu city in NS. 774 (A.D. 1654).

Lakhe Jatra

In the genealogy the Lakhe Jatra is described to be a Buddhist ceremony which had become prevalent in honour of Shakya Muni Buddha having obtained a victory over Namuchi Mara (or Cupid) when the latter came to distract his attention, while he was sitting under a Bodhi tree in profound meditation for the purpose of becoming a Buddha. After his victory Brahma and other gods came to pay their respects to Buddha, for which reason the gods are represented in this Jatra (Wright, p. 104). This Jatra was discontinued for some time and was revived by King Gunakama Deva.

Lakshmi Barma Bihar

One King Lakshmikama Deva is described in the genealogy to have worshipped the daughter of one Banda of Lakshmi Barman Bihar near Patan palace as Kumari (Wright, p. 105).

Amoghapash Lokeshor

Lokeshwara or Padmapani Bodhisattwa

A legend contained in the genealogical work (Wright, pp. 93-102) gives the origin and the entry of the cult of Lokeshwara or Padmapani Bodhisattwa or Matsyendranath in Nepal. The source says that in this universe Niranjana and other Buddhas, whose forms are Satchit (existence and thought), in order to create the world, produced the five elements and took the form and names of the five Buddhas. The fourth Buddha, Padmapani Bodhisattwa, the son of Amitabha, sprung from his mind, and sat in a state of deep meditation, called Loka Sansarjana or the creation of the universe.

The almighty Adi Buddha then named him as Lokeshwara to create the universe. He then created Brahma and other gods and because he sat in the Sukhavati Bhuvana heaven, and watched attentively Brahma and the other gods, to ensure their protection, he was called Aryavalokiteshwara Padmapani Bodhisattwa. This Buddha came to Banga (or Bengal) from his abode where Shiva came to learn from him Yoga Jnana (union with the supreme being by means of profound meditation). After learning the Yoga, Shiva returned to his home with Parvati but one night Parvati asked him to explain her the knowledge learnt from Aryavalokiteshwara. When Shiva was explaining Yoga, Parvati fell asleep and Aryavalokiteshwara Padmapani Bodhisattwa transformed himself into a fish and performed the part of a listener. Parvati at last awoke, and on being questioned showed that she had not heard all that Shiva had explained. This made Shiva suspect that someone else was listening, and he exclaimed - 'whoever is lurking here must appear, or I will curse him.' On this Lokeshwara appeared in his true form,

Nrityanath Lokeshor

and Shiva falling at his feet making many apologies, was forgiven. From that day Lokeshwara was called Matsyendranath because he had taken the form of a fish to listen Shiva's explanation of Yoga knowledge.

Gorakhnath then knew that Matsyendranath daily resorted to the Kamani mountain but it was difficult to go there to meet the almighty. Then he thought a way to bring Matsyendranath in Nepal. He would catch the nine Nagas and confine them so that they would be unable to bring rain and causing a great drought and then Matsyendranath would come to the relief of the people. This Gorakhnath did and the people faced a great drought which made the people and the King Bara Deva. Once King Bara Deva overheard a conversation between Bandhu Datta and his wife concerning the solution of the drought. Having heard that his father Narendra Deva, who had become a Bhikshu and lived in his Bihar, can suggest the means of fighting drought, Bara Deva went to ask his father who returned home with him. They sent for Bandhu Datta and asked him about the means. The priest agreed to help only with the help of Narendra Deva. Then the two accompanied by one gardener and his wife came to Dolama and performed a religious rite of reciting secret syllable ten million times. Then Narendra Deva and the gardener woman remained there keeping a sacred pot (Kalasha). Bandhu Datta then performed another rite to summon the help of goddess Jogambara Jnana Dakini who became pleased and promised her assistance to his task. Bandhu Datta gained power to rescue Karkotak Naga from the grasp of Gorakhnath and carried him to Kapotal mountain. Whenever they had to cross a river or a bad road he took out Karkotak who carried them over it. After encountering many hurdles they reached Kapotal mountain and Bandhu Datta began a rite to invoke Arya Avalokiteshwara who came to know the drought of Nepal and determined to go to Nepal to protect the country. Aryavalokiteshwara gave much insight into his secrets and disappeared to reside with a Yakshini whom he called his mother and named Gyana Dakini from being created by Maya or delusion. But when Avalokiteshwara was about to go to Bandhu Datta his mother tried to prevent him but transformed himself into a black bee entered into the sacred pot (Kalasha) three times. But Narendra Deva could not shut the pot as ordered by the Acharya because he was sleeping during the invoking rite. But at last Bandhu Datta, giving Narendra Deva a touch with his feet, awoke him and caused the mouth of the pot to be closed. Then Bandhu Datta worshipped Matsyendranath in the form of a bee. King Narendra Deva determined in his mind to slay Bandhu Datta because he had touched him with his foot.

After this, Gyana Dakini with numerous gods, Yakshas, and devils came to attack Bandhu Datta who, being hard pressed called all the gods of Nepal to his assistance. The Nepalese gods went to Bandhu Datta and consulted to decide that the office of ruler and protector of Nepal should be entrusted to Matsyendranath. Bandhu Datta on his part promised to send occasional offerings to Gyana Dakini and other gods who had objected to Matsyendranatha's being taken to Nepal. Having thus satisfied every one, Bandhu Datta worshipped Aryavalokiteshwara in the Kalasha, according to the Dasha Karma of ten ceremonies observed on the birth of a child.

When Bandhu Datta was about to depart Gyana

Dakini asked what road he intended to go back to Nepal. He replied,by any way, they liked to point out. The gods and devils, who had come from the Kamarupa mountain, then said that he should take the god by the way of Kamarupa, and that he should leave marks along the road to enable the god to return by the same route. For this purpose, they said, they would give him a quantity of deodar seeds to scatter as he went along Bandhu Datta agreed to this, but stipulated that the god should only return as far as the deodar trees produced from this seed extended. The gods, bhutas, pretas, Pishachas, Yakshas, and gandharvas agreed to this; whereupon, by means of a mantra, Bandhu Datta parched the seeds and carried away the god, scattering the parched seeds as he went, and thus he reached the Kotpal mountain (Chobhar).

After propitiating the gods, daityas, gandharvas, Yakshas, Rakshasas etc. who had come from the Kamarupa mountain Bandhu Datta sent them back. Then he worshipped the Kalasha in which Aryavalokiteshwara was, and invoking all the deities of Nepal, he held a great Jatra on the banks of Bagmati river, as he entered Nepal and now he scattered the unparched devadaru seeds along the road by which they entered the country.

During the Jatra, the Kalasha in which Aryavalokiteshwara was carried by four Bhairavas, (Hayagriva, Harasiddhi, Lutabaha of Pachhilu village and Tyanga). Brahma swept the road, reciting the Vedas, Vishnu blew Shankha, Mahadeva sprinkled Kalasha water on the road, Indra held an umbrella, Yamaraja lighted the incense, Varuna sprinkled water from a Shankha, and rain fell, Kubera scattered riches, Agni displayed light, Nairitya removed obstacles, Vayu held the flag, Ishana scared away devils. In this manner all the gods showed their respect while bringing Aryavalokiteshwara Matsyendra Natha. These gods however, were not visible to any except Bandhu Datta and Narendra Deva. The people only saw Bandhu Datta, Narendra Deva, the gardener and his wife, and the gods in the shape of birds and beasts.

A plentiful rain now fell in Nepal. When the procession reached a certain spot they sat down to rest, and here Harisiddhi Bhairava, in the shape of a dog, barked and said 'bu' which Bandhu Datta explained to Narendra Deva to mean 'birth place', and that they were to consider that Matsyendra Natha was born on this spot.

In honour of the gods, who came so far in company with them, and of the spot thus mysteriously pointed out by the dog, Bandhu Datta, after consultation with Narendra Deva determined to build a town and name it Amarapura and here he placed the Kalasha containing Aryavalokiteshwara Matsyendra Natha. They then appointed two priests to worship him in turn. One of these was a distant cousin of Bandhu Datta, and a descendant of a priest of Swayambhu, who lived in the Tairatna Bihar. The other was also a resident of Te Bahal. They were assigned to these lands for their maintenance.

Then the three met King Bira Deva and decided that a Rath-Yatra would be instituted with an image of the god. But the three wanted to have the festival performed in his town. Bandhu Datta wanted it at Kantipur, Narendra Deva at Bhaktapur and the gardener at Lalitpur. Disputing on the matter they arrived at Ikhatol in Patan and seeing a great crowd of people they agreed to abide by the decision of the oldest man there. Therefore, they called the headman of the whole of Patan, and having put sacred things on his head, asked for the decision. The headman thought - there is no town where Narendra Deva lived, nor where Bandhu Datta lives. These three people have all taken equal pains and trouble, but it is Narendra Deva who has been put to expense. However, I shall give my decision in favour of Lalitpur, because it is a large town with many inhabitants and King Bara Deva has come from Madhyalakhu to reside here, and besides it is my own city. In showing this partiality, and doing injustice to Narendra Deva, I shall, however, I am sure, be swallowed up by the earth. Having formed this resolution he caused seven Ukhals to be brought and piled one upon another. He then ascended to the top of them and spoke thus: "Hear, O Bandhu Datta Acharya Narendra Deva, Malakar and all you people ! Anything to be done for Padmapani Aryavalokiteshwara Matsyendra Natha should be referred to Mangal Bhatta where reside gods of the whole three worlds. Having thus spoken he was swallowed up by the earth, and so died. The spot is still known to the people of Patan (near Pode Tol south of Mangal Bazar).

The audience, being contented with the decision went to the Bihar where Sunayashri Mishra once lived as a Bhikshu as the spot was considered to be sacred. After that they did a sacred rite of Purashcharana at Chobhu. Then taking possession of one-third of the Bihar built by Sunaya Shri Mishra, they caused an image to be made of Aryavalokiteshwara Matsyendra Nath. After consecration the image was carried to Amarpura where he was worshipped. After this a ritual was done the spirit of the god was transferred to the image. This image was made of earth brought from the Himayapido mound (Mhaipi, near Lazimpat) with the earth of which also the Swayambhu chaitya was built by Prachanda Deva in accordance with the directions of Shantikar Acharya. Jogambara Gyana Dakini was first worshipped there to take earth from this mound.

Then Bandhu Datta established the rites of worship in this order - The image of the deity was brought from Amarpur, when the sun was in the northern hemisphere, and kept in a temple built in Tau Bihar. He was bathed on the Ist of Chaitra Badi. On the 8th he was put in the sun. On the 12th and 13th the Dasha Karma ceremonies were performed. On the Ist of Baishakh Sudi he was put on the Ratha (chariot) and after being taken round the city of Lalitpur he was conveyed back to Amarpur (Bugmati) when the sun was in the southern Hemisphere.

When the Ratha Jatra of Matsyendra Natha started in Patan the Ratha Jatras of Dhalacche Lokeshwara, Swatha Narayana and others, which used to take place in Lalitpur were discontinued except that of Minanatha Dharmaraj, who is Junior Macchindra. From this year too the Ratha Jatra of Chaubahal (or Chobhar) was discontinued, which used to take place in Deva Patan every year, because the Ratha, in returning from Deva Patan, was sunk in the Danagal river.

The Bandhu went to meet Narendra Deva to ask him whether all his wishes had been accomplished. The latter thanked Bandhu Datta for his perseverence to bring the Lord and he is quite satisfied with his endeavour. Bandhu Datta again asked him to tell if any of his wishes are not yet fulfilled but Narendra Deva did not state any such. Then Bandhu Datta reminded him of the event of his touching Narendra

Deva by his feet and the latter's determination to kill him. Narendra Deva begged Bandhu Datta to forget. The Acharya told him that it was not from his ill-will that he mentioned this but that it was incumbent on him to carry out any resolution made at the moment when he was in the presence of the Lord Bandhu Datta. Then he made a figure of himself with boiled rice, at which Narendra Deva struck, and thus accomplished his vow but the same night he died and being absolved, was incorporated with the right foot of Matsyendra Natha. Hearing Bandhu Datta's death Narendra Deva too was absolved and incorporated with the left foot of the deity. For this reason one going to see Matsyendra Natha looks at his feet, to see the two devotees - Narendra Deva and Bandhu Datta.

Seeing such devotion of Narendra Deva and Bandhu Datta the people became very much attached to the worship of Aryavalokiteshwara Matsyendra Natha, who in return always gives plentiful rain and protects the people. The Lord was brought to Nepal in Kali Gata year 3623.

King Bara Deva is reported in the genealogy to have reintroduced the Harisiddhi dance, started by Bikramajit. But he made a rule that the dance should be first performed at Matsyendra Natha's temple.

Lokeshvar - Shiva Sculpture

There is a stone sculpture in the small museum in Swayambhu which is inscribed and dated A.D. 1677 (Nepal Era 797). Buddhist deity Lokeshvara takes the central position in the sculpture, while in a small portion inside figures of Shiva and Parvati are depicted. This appears to be an extraordinary

Bajrapani

example of Buddhist - Shaivite cult.

Maha Buddha Temple

The famous Maha Buddha temple at Patan is said to have been built by one Jivaraj. A legend is also recorded in the genealogical work on the origin of this temple and Jivaraja's life. The legend (Wright, pp. 138-39, 141) goes thus:

"During King Amara Malla's reign there lived a Bauddhacharya, by name Abhayaraja, clever and devoted to his religion. He had three wives two of whom were fruitful, one had two sons and the other four. He then married fourth wife, and seeing that his elder sons were displeased at this, he left the wife with four sons at Onkuli Bihar, and the other with sons at a house which he had recently built, and he himself went to Bauddha Gaya with his newly married wife. He remained there three years as a devotee of Buddha. One day he heard a voice from the sky, telling him that Maha Buddha had accepted his service and worship, and that he should now return to his home, where Maha Buddha would come to visit him, and where he would receive the royal favour. The voice also told him that she who spoke was Bidyadhari Devi, a handmaid of Maha Buddha.

At this time, however, Abhayaraja's wife was pregnant, and they therefore could not undertake the journey. In due season, a son was born, and named Bauddhaju. After this they returned home taking with them a model Bauddha image from that place.

On arriving home, Abhayaraja built a three-storied Buddhist temple and erected a Bauddha with an image of Shakya Muni, in which he placed the model image. To the east of the temple in his former house, he built an Agama, and placed there an image of Bidyadhari Devi. King Amara Malla told him that as his (the Raja's) father had appointed Madhana, Abhayaraja's father, Dittha Naikya, to superintend the making of price. The king then appointed him to the same post.

During the reign of King Sadashiva Malla, Jivaraja, the son of Bauddhaju, the son of Abhayaraja, the great devotee of Buddha, who was born at Bodh Gaya, visited that holy place, and after returning home built a large temple like the one at Gaya, consisting entirely of Buddhist images. It was named Maha Buddha Devalaya.

This Jivaraja, after performing a great puja, and thinking of taking some prasada of the Maha Buddha to the Lamas of the north, went to the Lama of Sikkim and told him how he built the great temple.

The Lama gave him a plateful of gold, and he returned home and made golden shafts for the chariot of Matsyendra Natha, and assigned land for their maintenance, which is called Lutham Guthi.

Jaya Muni, the son of Jivaraja, seeing that the Bauddhamargis of Nepal were deteriorating for want of clever Pandits, well versed in the Buddhist scriptures, and for want also of good books, disguised himself as Dandi (Hindu mendicant) and went to Kashi where he studied grammar etc. and then returned to Nepal, with a great collection of Buddhist scriptures. Thus he promoted the Bauddha religion and himself became famous as the great Pandit of Maha Buddha."

Mahamandap Hill

In genealogical work it is said that Manjushri Bodhisattwa had come from Maha China in Treta Yuga and had stayed at the Mahamandap hill (Wright, p. 51). This Mahamandap hill is situated about one mile east of Bhadgaon. It is also called Manjushri Than. Here a chaitya of Manjushri stands.

Mahankal, Tundikhel

Lichchavi King Gunakama Deva - III is said to have built the Mahankal temple of Tundikhel in cooperation of Saswata Vajra Vajracharya of Mantra Siddhi Mahavihar (or Saval Bahal, Batu Tol). It is believed now that once (Treta Yuga?) the deity Mahankal Bhairava was crossing Nepal from Tibet to go to Kashi but Shasvata Bajra Bajracharya had attracted him through mystic power and placed him in an earthern mound. On the Ashadha Krishna Tritiya day the mound was opened to find an image of the deity. Since the deity was captivated to live in Nepal his image is always bound in iron chains. The important occasion of finding the deity is honoured as a festive day called 'Bandi Mahan Puja' on the Ashadh Krishna Tritiya day when the deity is specially worshipped.

Mahasattwa

In the genealogical work Mahasattwa is described as a son of Panchala or Panauti King Maharatha's son who had offered his own flesh to a hungry tigress and thus acquired spiritual merits (Wright, pp. 73-74). When Shakya Simha Buddha visited here he showed his disciple's ornaments belonging to himself buried under a chaitya. The Buddha is said there to have described Mahasattwa as his former birth.

Mana Deva

One medieval King Mana Deva is described in the genealogy to have abdicated in favour of his eldest son and lived as a Bandya in a Bihar. This Bihar, having on it numerous Chakras was called Chakra Bihar (Wright, p. 109).

Mani Chaitya

Mani chaitya is said to have originated from the virtue of King Manichuda's penance and his donation of his Mani Jewel on his forehead (Wright, p. 69).

Mani Chaitya

One King Bira Deva of ancient period is also recorded in the genealogy to have built a Mani chaitya besides others in an underground tank after establishing the city of Lalit Pattan (Wright, p. 90).

Manichura, King

It is mentioned in the genealogical work (Wright, p. 69) that Manichura, King of Saketa (Ayodhya) had performed penance and the Nirguna Yajna sacrifice at a mountain north-east of the valley. After performing the sacrifice he donated the Mani or Jewel on his forehead and these ten things sprang up from his virtue:

1. Manichura mountain
2. Manilinga
3. Manirohini
4. Manitalava
5. Mani Jogini

Arapchana Manjushri

6. Mani Chaitya
7. Manidhara
8. Mani Ganesha
9. Mani Mahakala
10. Manimati River

Manju Pattan City

Manjushri Bodhisattwa is credited in the genealogical work to have built an ever first town in Kathmandu Valley named after him. This city extended from Swayambhu to Guheshwari (Wright, p. 51). The first settlers of the city were Manjushri's disciples as householders and mendicants. For the mendicants he had also built a Vihar. He himself made the first King named Dharmakara.

Manjushri Bodhisattwa

The genealogical work relates the legend of Manjushri Bodhisattwa (Wright, pp. 51-52). Accordingly in Treta Yuga Manjushri Bodhisattwa came here from Mahachin (or China) and stayed on Mahamandap hill (east of Bhadgaon) for three nights and saw the Swayambhu light. He then thought of cutting a passage through the mountains to drain the Naga Hrad and went towards south and placed his two consort goddesses Barada and Mokshada on Phullochacha (Phulchoki) and the other on Dhyanochacha mount while he remained in the middle. He then cut through the mountain which he called Kotwal (or Kotwaldwar Chobhar) and let the water run out. When the water started running out Nagas (serpents) and other animals living in it went out. But Manjushri persuaded Naga King Karkotaka to remain and on the Vaishakha Sankranti (Mesha Sankranti) day he appointed him to live in a lake (called as Taudaha) and empowered him the authority over the wealth of the valley.

After that event Manjushri got a vision of Swayambhu in the form of Bishwarupa on the Kartik Purnima day. Again on Pausha Krishna 9th day he discovered Guhyeshwari in the form of Bishwarupa. He also made the Padma or Swayambhu hill and built the Manju Pattan city expanding from Swayambhu to Guhyeshwari. He planted trees near Guhyeshwari and peopled the Manju Pattan town with those of his disciples who wished to live as Grihasthas or householders, and to those who wished to live as Bhikshus, he allotted a Vihara. He then installed a king named Dharmakara in the Manju Pattan city and returned to his country, China.

Manjushri Chaitya

After Manjushri Bodhisattwa's return to China his disciples had built a chaitya, just west of the Swayambhu hill which was named after Manjushri (Wright, p. 51). Since the chaitya was built on the Magha Shukla Panchami day, the event is commemorated even today by offering prayers and worship on that spot.

Manko Bahal Patan

In a later chronological work (Devamala Vamshavali, p. 59) one King Mana Deva who had become the King of Lalitpur (i.e. Patan) had built the Manko Bahal after consulting Bauddha Acharyas who were well versed in Mantras. A tunnel was built under the Bahal and a chaitya was built and serpent gods (Nagas) were also placed there. All these acts were done to have rains in drought cases when Bajracharyas would enter into the temple according to prescribed rules.

Matrirajya

The Lagankhel chaitya is also called Matrirajya (Wright, p. 80).

Mhaipi Azima

The shrine of Mhaipi Azima is otherwise known as Yogambara Jnanashri among Buddhists, Hindus worship her as Chamunda chandika or Mahalakshmi.

Mokshada Goddess

Manjushri Bodhisattwa is said in the genealogical work to have placed his consort goddess Mokshada on the Dhyanochacha (Dhyamacho) mountain top (Wright, p. 51). She is also taken as Saraswati or the goddess of learning.

It is amazing to find a traditional saying that the Rudrayani Devi of Khokana village (southern part of the valley) is same as Dhyanacho Maju or Chunni Mai of Dhyamacho hill. Rudrayani Devi of Khokana village was established by King Amara Malla following the supernatural advice given to the king in his dream after he had settled the 700 houses city of Khokana. The famous dance of Rudrayani was also initiated since then.

Naga Hrada or Kali Hrada

Legends say that the Kathmandu Valley was covered by water and thus a lake was formed. In Swayambhu Purana we find the lake named Naga Hrada or Kali Hrada (SP. 131). There 33 crores of Nagas or serpents resided. The genealogy states that the lake was created by Adhi Buddha.

Nagarjunapada

Nagarjunapada is recorded in the genealogical work to have made a cave on the Jatamatrochcha mountain (now called Nagarjuna hill) where he had placed an image of Akshobhya Buddha to worship Swayambhu. As the water filled the valley, it rose up to the navel of this image, whereupon Nagarjuna caught the Naga that was playing in the water and making it rise, and confined him in the cave. Whatever water was required in this cave was supplied by this Naga to the present day, and for this reason the Naga is called Jalapurita. Nagarjunapada also made an earthern chaitya, and composed many Tantric texts, and discovered many gods. He died in the cave. The mountain then became known as Nagarjuna, and is considered to be very sacred. People who are anxious to obtain salvation leave orders with their relatives to send their skullbone to this mountain, where it is thrown high into the air, then buried, and a chaitya built over it (Wright, pp. 63 64).

At Bangmati in the courtyard of the Matsyendranatha there is an image which is identified as Nagarjuna, the famous Buddhist scholar.

Naga Worship

In the genealogy a legend is recorded about a drought and famine because the King Gunakama Deva had committed incest and the gods were displeased and had sent drought and famine in Nepal. The king then having been initiated by Shantikara Acharya brought the Nine Naga serpents under his control and caused them to give a plentiful rain. When the king was performing the ceremony to summon the Nagas, Karkotaka, who lived in the Nagadaha, did not come readily but the other eight did. Upon this Shantikara Acharya gave Gunakama Deva some dubgrass and kund flowers through the virtue of which he jumped into the tank, and catching hold of Karkotaka, made him a prisoner. On his way home he became tired, and sat down to rest at the foot of the Swayambhu mount. This place is still marked by an image of Karkotaka Naga, at the south-east corner of the mount, called Nagashila. The road by which the king brought the Naga was called Nagabato. When Gunakama Deva brought Karkotaka before Shantikara Acharya all the Nagas worshipped him and they each gave him a likeness of themselves (paintings), drawn with their own blood, and declared that whenever there was a drought hereafter, plentiful rain would fall as soon as these pictures are worshipped (Wright, p. 56).

Nairatma Yogini

Newar Buddhists worship Guhyeshwari as Nairatma Yogini.

Namo Buddha

Namo Buddha (or Nammudha) chaitya stands on a hill which is said to be named Gandhakuta Parvata.

Shakya Simha Buddha is described in the genealogical work to have visited the Namo Buddha mountain about 12 miles south-east of Bhadgaon, outside the valley (Wright, pp. 73-74). There he discovered and showed his disciples certain ornaments belonging to himself used by him in his former birth, buried under a chaitya. In his former birth Buddha was born to the King Maharatha of Panauti or Panchala named as Prince Mahasattwa. He had buried his ornaments after destroying himself by giving his own flesh to eat to a hungry tigress. Buddha replaced these ornaments as they were and repaired the chaitya.

Namo Buddha is also known to the Tibetans who call it as Takmo Luijin (Nangba Sange, p. 111).

A drama in Newari language entitled 'Mahasattwopakhyana' is said to have been composed by King Rajendra Bikram Shah. It is dated A.D. 1831.

In 1872 Jang Bahadur had restored the land grants made to the temple of Namobuddha which were confiscated by government and given in jagirs to soldiers (Padmajang-Life of Janga Bahadur, p. 285). Jang Bahadur also paid the arrears due to the time of confiscation of the land of the temple.

Nangba Sange

According to Colonel Santabir Lama the Tamangs, Kagate, Yolmali, Khamboli, Thakali, Mananga, Holange, Sing Syakpa, Sherpa, Gurung and some sections of Newars are the followers of Mahayana Nangba Sange Sangha (Nangba Sange, p. Ga, Intro.).

Ne Muni

In the genealogical work (Wright, p. 58) one Ne Muni is described to have named the country after his name. He is described there to have performed devotions at the junction of the Bagmati and Keshabati, and, by the blessing of Swayambhu and Bajra Jogini, he instructed the people in the true path of virtue and religion and also ruled over the country.

Nepali Buddhism.

In the genealogical work we find a statement made by Gorakhnatha which offers a general view on the Buddhist deities professed in the valley including Aryavalokiteshvara. This statement (Wright, pp. 93-94) goes as follows:

> During King Bara Deva's reign Gorakhnath came to Nepal and reflected thus: In this universe Niranjana and other Buddhas, whose forms are Satchitta (existence and thought) in order to create the world, produced the Pancha-tattwas (five elements), and took the form and names of the five Buddhas. The fourth Buddha, Padmapani Bodhisattwa, the son of Amitabha sprung from his mind, sat in a state of Samadhi (deep meditation), called Loka sansarjana (creation of the world). The Adi Buddha then named him Lokeshwara and gave him the duty of creating the world. He then created Brahma and other gods and because he sat in Sukhavati heaven and watched attentively Brahma and other gods, to ensure their protection, he was called Aryavalokiteshwara Padmapani Bodhisattwa. This Buddha went from Sukhavati to a place called Banga (Bengal), where Shiva came to learn from him Yoga Jnana (union with the supreme being by means of profound meditation). Shiva, after learning Yoga, was returning home with Parvati, when one night he stayed on the sea-shore, and Parvati asked him to repeat to her what he had learned from Padmapani. He did so, but Parvati fell asleep when Shiva was explaining and Aryavalokiteswara Padmapani Bodhisattwa

Pancha Buddha (Five Main Buddhas)

Aksobhya

Amoghasiddhi

Vairochana

Ratna Sambhava

Amitabhava

transformed himself into a fish and performed the part of a listener. Parvati at last awoke, and on being questioned showed that she had not heard all that Shiva had recounted. This made Shiva suspect that some one else was listening, and he exclaimed 'whoever is lurking in this place must appear, or I will curse him. On this Lokeshvara appeared in his true form, and Shiva falling at his feet making many apologies, was forgiven. From that day the Lokeshvara, on account of his having taken the form of a fish, was known as Matsyendra Natha.

Nepal, Meaning of

According to Buddhist Newars 'Ne' means the sender to paradise' who is Swayambhu Adi Buddha and 'Pala' means 'cherished' (Hodgson, Essays, p. 51).

Nhul Bahal

The Bandas of Pingala Bahal had removed to Patan then they brought the deity of their Bihar to Patan. The then King Bhaskara Deva built Nhul Bahal to keep the deity did not approve this Bihar then the king again built another Bihar Hema Barma Bihar (Wright, p. 106).

Niglihawa Ashokan Pillar

An Ashokan pillar was found in Niglihawa in A.D. 1893. The inscription on this pillar records that King Ashoka, in his 14th year of his reign, personally worshipped the Stupa of Buddha Konakamana, and added to it for the second time.

Oku Bahal

It is called as "Shiva Deva Samskarita Omkuli

Shri Rudra Varma Mahavihar". Omkuli here means south-east quarter in Newari language i.e. its situation towards south-east of the Patan Durbar Square (Ratna Jyoti Shakya, Omkuli Shri Rudra Varma Mahavihar, 1980, p. 8).

The following named 30 Buddhist Viharas are said to be under the jurisdiction of Oku Bahal (Ratna Jyoti Shakya, Op. Cit. pp. 18-19):

1. Omkuli Vahi or Uba Vahi
2. Bodhi Mandap Vihar or Mahabauddha
3. Khandchuka Vihar or Twayavaha
4. Mitravarna Vihar or Twayavaha
5. Valadhara Gupta Vihar or Yashhya Vaha
6. Devadatta Vihar or Nandavaha
7. Amritavarna Vihar or Nuga Nhuvaha
8. Jayashri Vihar or Jothevaha
9. Jayavardhana Vihar or Jativaha
10. Samantabhadra Vihar or Paluvaha
11. Kanakavarna Vihar or Kanivaha
12. Padmavarna Vihar or Jyathavaha
13. Rupavarna Vihar or Nauvaha
14. Sumangala Vihar or Yanga Vaha
15. Ichya Vihar or Ichyevaha
16. Purnachandra Vihar or Dunevaha
17. Nava Vihar or Nhu Vaha
18. Simhachuka Vihar or Sikucha Vaha
19. Himavarna Vihar or Hitiphusvaha
20. Dhanavir Vihar or Jyatha Dhanavaha

21. Amritavarna Vihar or Nuga Dhana Vaha
22. Yatalibi Vihar or Yotalivi
23. Vasuvarna Vihar or Vasu Vaha
24. Tadhanlivi Vihar or Tadhanlivi Vaha
25. Hiranyalava Vihar or Teja Bhajudhana Vaha
26. Ratnalava Vihar or Tajur Bhimaraj Vaha
27. Kutasingha Vihar or Tajur Bhimaraj Vaha
28. Kulachaitya Vihar or Kulachaitya Vaha
29. Dhanavajra Vihar or Dhana Vaha
30. Jayamangala Vihar or Tanavaha

Padma Deva Sanskrita Bihara

One person Padma Deva is said in the genealogical work to have built a temple for Dharmaraj Minanatha Lokeshwara, in which he placed images of Samanta Bhadra Bodhisattwa and Padmapani Bodhisattwa together with those of other Bodhisattwas, gods, planets and etc. This is called the Padma Deva Sanskrita Bihar, and its history is inscribed on a stone fixed in a chaitya in front of this Lokeshwara. This was during King Yaksha Malla's reign (Wright, p. 128).

Padma Mountain

Manjushri Bodhisattwa is again credited to have made the hill Padma, the Swayambhu hill as we know from the genealogical work (Wright, p. 51).

Panchadan or Banda Yatra

One mythical King Vikrama Sena is credited to have instituted the Banda Yatra as recorded by a genealogical work on temples (Yogi Narahari Nath

- Devamala Vamshavali, VS. 2013, p. 102). According to the said source the origin of this festival is quoted below in transalation:

> The illustrious King Vikrama Sena brought Maheshvar Thakur, a learned man on six Shastras (classics) from southern country. As counselled by Maheshvar Thakur the King made a rule in Kaligata year 2973 that Buddhist should observe a Bauddha Yatra (Buddhist festival) during Shravan Shukla Pratipada to Bhadra Krishna Amavasya. And, on Bhadra Krishna Trayodashi day they should give alms of grains. To observe that rule a wooden pavillion was built at Marutol (near the Kasthamandapa). People gave alms sitting on the pavillion which was covered by wooden beams. Later during King Vrisha Deva's time a Guthi endowment was instituted for the same purpose which is continued uptill now. Since there had been wooden beams in this locality, so it was called Kathmandu.
>
> But at present Bauddha Yatra commences from Shravan Shukla Pratipada to Bhadra Krishna Amavasya and only on Bhadra Krishna Trayodashi alms giving to the Bandas is observed sitting on the wooden pavillion (or only timbers).

In Kathmandu the alms giving custom is continued on Bhadra Krishna Trayodashi. But in Patan it is observed on Shravan Shukla Ashtami day. The Panchadan is a part of a month-long Bauddha-Yatra or Gunla-Dharma pilgrimage-festival.

In genealogical work we find a legend relating to the Panchadana ritual (Wright, pp. 57-58). According to the legend in the Satya Yuga there was a city named Dipavati named after Dipankara

Buddha's image, in which lived a virtuous king whose name was Sarvananda, supposed to be an incarnation of Buddha. When visiting once Guhyeshvari, he was pleased with the place, and built a palace and fixed his abode there and also built a Bihar adjacent to it and gave it to Bhikshus to reside. He also built a chaitya in front of his palace, and appointed a day for fasting in honour of it.

One day he wished to give presents and alms to beggars and fixed days for that purpose on the anniversaries of the beginning of the Yugas.

At this time there was an old woman who also gave alms, and Dipankar Buddha appeared in corporal form and took her alms before those of the king. The king upon this asked him why he preferred to take the old woman's alms first, and he answered that the grain given by her had been collected with much greater labour than the Raja's gold. This set the king thinking, and seeing a blacksmith working hard with his hammer, so that he was all covered with sweat, he went to work along with him. He remained working there for two months, and brought good luck to his host. The money which he earned he spent in purchasing gifts for the beggars and fixed the 8th of Shravan Shukla as the day for distributing them. Dipankar Buddha again appeared, after taking his alms, blessed him, and said that the fame of this meritorious act would spread to the end of the world, and that in Kali Yuga salvation would be obtained only through Buddha. The king then placed an image of Dipankar in his palace. The Bihar which he had built previously to this, in front of which he had made a chaitya, became known by the name of Dipavati, and people celebrate the anniversary of the 8th day of the Shravan Shukla by worshipping Buddha.

An occasion of Banda Jatra is recorded in the genealogy for the year A.D. 1649 in Patan. According to the said source (Wright, p. 163) Gopi of Ikhancche Tol, Dam Bandya of Slako Bahal and Madhava Chitrakar of Kothosatigla had prepared to make a Banda Jatra; but as the King Siddhi Narasimha did not allow them bring the deity, they made no rejoicing, but only gave the alms. The king also did not go to the Jatra.

In 1877 Daniel Wright had noted the 'Banra Jatra' as quoted below:

> "This festival takes place twice a year, on the 8th of sawan and 13th of Bhadau. The Banras (Bandas) or priests of the Bauddha-margi Newars go about from house to house and receive a handful of rice or grain at each. This is done in commemoration of their ancestors having been Bhikshus or mendicant priests, who lived on alms and followed no trade.
>
> The Newars on these occasions decorate their shops and houses with pictures, flowers etc, and women sit in front with large baskets of rice and grains, which they dispense in handfuls to the Banras as they pass.
>
> A wealthy Newar may get up a private Banra Jatra at any time, if he pleases, but it is an expensive amusement, as he has to make large presents to the first Banra who gets his foot over the threshold of the house. If the king is invited to this Jatra, he must be presented with a silver throne, umbrella and cooking utensils" (D. Wright, History of Nepal, p. 25).

Pau Bahal

According to the genealogical work King Pratap Malla of Kathmandu had placed a painting, representing figures engaged in churning the ocean in the Pau Bahal, and he directed that it should be taken out on great festival days (Wright, p. 148). The king is also said to have assigned a trust for the purpose.

Pausha Krishna Navami

In genealogical work (Wright, p. 51) it is stated that Manjushri Bodhisattwa had discovered Guhyeshwari as Bishwarupa on the Pausha Krishna Navami.

Phullochcha Mountain

The mountain from where Bishwabhu Buddha had offered one lakh of flowers to Swayambhu light. The offering of flower was a memorable event hence the mountain was named by the said Buddha as Pullochcha (high with flowers) (Wright, p. 50). It is now called as Phulchoki above Godabari region towards south-east of the Kathmandu Valley.

Pingal Bahal Kot

We find a legend in the genealogy (Wright, pp. 69-70) on the building of the Pingala Bahal Kot by one Queen named Pingala, disgraced by her husband. She is said there to have performed penance by fasting at Guhyeshwari. On Guhyeshwari command she had built Pingala Bahal and placed there images of gods and goddesses. When Pingala Rani returned to her own country along with her husband she had left Pingala Bahal Kot in charge of Buddhist priests to worship the deities installed there (Wright, p. 81).

Remains of this Bahal is situated at Battisputali near Pashupati.

Pintha Bihara

This Bihar was built by Sunaya Shri Mishra's disciples who had come to meet their Guru from Kapilbastu (Wright, p. 78). Here are preserved specimens of a large rice grain without husk and rice with husk as they grew during the old times. The so called grains are as big as small nutmegs and are exhibited in the month of Shravan.

Pongal Bahal

In the genealogical work we find mention of one Pongala Bahal where King Narendra Deva had sent his eldest son Padma Deva to become a Bandya where at one time six hundred Bandyas lived (Wright, p. 93).

Pratapa Malla Builds Temples at Swayambhu

The genealogical work describes Kathmandu King Pratapa Malla building temples at Swayambhu:

"During the reign of Mahipatendra Malla, Pratapa Malla placed a large Bajra (thunderbolt) in the Dharma Dhatu Mandala in front of Akshobhya Buddha, on the eastern side of Swayambhu in NS 788 (A.D. 1668). To the right and left of Swayambhu he built two temples, in which he put secret Agama Devatas" (Wright, p. 149).

The event is also corroborated by the said king's inscriptions standing at the site.

Prayag Pokhari

Prayag Pokhari i.e. a pond named after the

famous sacred place in Allahabad in India, is also a sacred place for the Newar Buddhists. The pond is believed to have been built by King Amshu Varman.

Puchchagra Chaitya

Buddha is said in the Vamshavali to have fixed his abode at Puchchagra chaitya (Wright, p. 73) which is located west of Swayambhu Stupa different than the Manjushri chaitya.

Rajendra Bikram Shah Repairs Swayambhu Stupa

King Rajendra Bikram Shah summoned a Lama from Lhasa to replace with a new shal beam the principal timber of Swayambhu Stupa, which had become rotton in 1820 A.D. (Wright, p. 181).

Rudra Deva

One medieval King Rudra Deva is described to have become a Buddhist in acquiring a knowledge of the elements (Wright, p. 109). He sincerely occupied himself in acquiring religious merit first as Bauddhacharya, then Mahayanikacharya and then Tribidhi Bodhi. After this he repaired the old Onkuli Bihar built by King Shiva Deva Varma, and after performing the Chuda Karma he lived in it as a Bandya, the sure way of obtaining salvation and thus he earned salvation. The king on one occasion sent an image of Dipankara Buddha to receive Pindapatra Dana instead of himself. He is also said to have kept a Guthi or trust, by name Bepar Madhi, in the name of his ancestors, Bama Deva, Harka Deva, Sadashiva Deva, Mana Deva, Narasimha Deva, Nanda Deva and of himself, for his own Bihar, in order that people living in it might be allowed to follow any trade.

To make this more secure, he informed his grandson Jaya Deva Malla of his having established this custom.

Rules Regarding Buddhism in Patan

Patan King Siddhi Narasimha Malla is recorded in the genealogical work to have issued some rules regarding some aspects of Buddhist activities in Patan. The statement of the said source is quoted below:

``In King Siddhi Narasimha Malla's reign the following Bihars existed:

1. *Jyestha Barna Tangal*
   built by Balarchana Deva
2. *Dharmakirti Tava*
   built by Bhuvanakara Barma
3. *Mayura Barma Bishnuksha*
   built by Shankara Deva
4. *Vaishna Barna Bihar*
   built by Baisdeva Barma
5. *Onkuli Rudra Barna Bihar*
   built by Shivadeva Barma
6. *Hakwa Bihar*
   built by Lakshmi Kalyan Barma
7. *Hiranya Barna Bihar*
   built by Bhaskara Deva Barma
8. *Jasodhara Buya Bihar*
   built by Bidyadhara Barma
9. *Chakra Bihar*
   built by Manadeva Barma
10. *Sakwa Bihar*

built by Indra Deva

11. *Datta Bihar*

built by Rudra Deva Garga Gotra

12. *Yancchu Bihar*

built by Baladhara Gupta

Among these the following five, namely, Bishnuksha, Onkuli, Gwakashe (Chakra), Sakwa and Yanchu had one Chief Naikya, who was the oldest among the five head Buddha-margis of the Bihars. The rest, namely, Tangal, Tava, Vishnabarna, Hakwa, Hiranya Barna, Jasodhara and Datta had each a separate Naike or Chief Buddha margi. The rank of Naike was conferred on the oldest Buddhist, and they were called Tathagatas.

Three Bihars - Wam Baha, Jyo Baha and Dhumbaha were established in King Siddhi Nara Simha Malla's reign.

The king called the Naikes of all these Biharas before him, and ordered them to establish the custom of Thapatwaya Guthi (a feast at which the Buddhists of Biharas assemble and choose their Naikes).

King Siddhi Nara Simha Malla called together the men of these 15 Biharas to make rules for their guidance, and directed that the order of their precedence should be fixed according to the order in which they arrived. The people of Dhum Bahal came first, but they were given only the third place. Those of Tangal Bihar remained first, and those of Tava second, on account of the antiquity of their Biharas. To the rest precedence was given according to the order in which they presented themselves.

Because Chau Bahal (Chobhar) and Kirtipur

were under the jurisdiction of Lalitpur, the Biharas of those places were amalgamated with the fifteen Bihars of Lalitpur. Another Bihar named Si Bihar was not amalgamated with these because it was built after the rules had been made by the king for their guidance, and Guthis had been assigned to them.

There were several old Biharas standing empty, which had existed before the founding of Lalitpur city, having been built by Nirbanik Banaprastha Bhikshus, who, after entering on the Grihastha life, had been removed to other places. Siddhi Nara Simha Malla gave these Biharas to other Bhikshus to live in. These new Bhikshus did not perform Homa when one of their family died. They began to have families, but still they did not perform this ceremony although they performed other ceremonies just like Grihasthas whose houses remain impure after a death without Homa ceremony, they must perform this ceremony.

The Yanpi Bihar, built by Sunaya Shri Mishra was Nirbanik (or the inhabitants did not marry); and as a Grihastha Acharya is required for performing the Homa, the king decided that one of the people from Dhum Bihar should act as a priest to perform the Homa in this Bihara.

The king next found that there were altogether 25 Nirbanik Biharas in the places under the jurisdiction of Lalitpur (i.e. Chobhar, Bangmati and Chapagaon); and in order to make rules for their guidance, he summoned all their Bhikshus. They did not, however, all come. The Bhikshus of only 15 Biharas came, namely of those lying on the left hand side of the route taken by Matsyendra Natha's Ratha during his Ratha-Yatra, and those to whom the king had given empty Biharas to live in.

He made a rule that the five oldest among their Bhikshus should be Naikes and should be called Pancha Buddhas, and he assigned a Guthi for their maintenance. He made rules for electing their Naikes or Headmen, and for performing the ceremonies after the death. He also ruled that the son of the oldest Naike Bhikshu should have the charge of the worship of the deities of all the Biharas; and he put a stop to the old custom, by which the worship was performed by the head Bhikshu of each Bihara. If this worshipper became one of the Pancha-Buddhas, then his son succeeded him in the performance of the worship. He also amalgamated those 15 Biharas with 15 mentioned before. Later he made separate rules for the remaining ten Biharas, which lay to the right hand of the route taken by Matsyendra Nathas' Ratha, and appointed headmen for them. The people of Lalitpur, as they could not worship such a number of Bhikshus, worshipped only two, the oldest among the Bhikshus of all the Biharas standing at the top of the public road, and the oldest of those standing at the foot of it (the oldest of the Bhikshus of the 15 Biharas first mentioned, and the other the oldest of the Bhikshus of the other ten Biharas).

The Banaprastha Biharas were called by some Bahi i.e. outside (in Sanskrit) because the Banaprastha Bhikshus did not live in cities, but in forests.

Bhima Malla, a Kaji (Minister) of Kathmandu King Lakshmi Narasimha Malla, having established 32 shops in Lhasa, Kuti etc., and having made a treaty with the ruler of Tibet, the merchants of Lalitpur began to go to trade there. Siddhi Narasimha Malla decided that the ceremony of purification of those who returned from Tibet should be superintended by the five old Naikes of Tava, Hakwa, Bu, Yam and

Bishnuksha Biharas but that the fees should go to the king. After undergoing this purification, the travelling merchants were readmitted into their caste. In one of the five Naikes during the ceremony his successor had to give a feast, undergo the usual ceremony for becoming a Naike before he could be admitted as one of them. This is called Twaya Guthi" (Wright, pp. 159-162).

In 1975 Lalitpur Bauddha Samaj Sudhar Samiti had convened a meeting of the members of 15 Bahals and 15 Bahils to reform the social problems among the Bajracharyas and Shakyas.

Sarbananda Pandit

King Bishnu Malla is said to have sent Sarbananda Pandit of Mahabuddha to Kwache Balkumari to perform Purascharana and Naga Sadhana when there was a drought and famine, after which rain fell (Wright, p. 170).

Shankaracharya's Visit

In the Buddhist type of genealogical work we find Shankaracharya's visit of the valley and his final victory over the Buddhists. The source (Wright, pp. 79-82) has given the following legend regarding Shankaracharya's activities in the valley:

> The incarnate Shankaracharya was born in the south of an immaculate Brahmani widow. In his six former incarnations he had been defeated in religious discussions by the Buddhists and had been cast into the fire. In his seventh incarnation there were no learned Buddhists but only 16 Bodhisattwas or novices who, hearing of Shankara's advent fled towards north to seek

refuge and died there. Shankara finding no clever Buddhists with whom to argue and hearing that the 16 Bodhisattwas had fled to Nepal, pursued him but could not find them. On his arrival in Nepal he did not find learned Buddhists though the four castes were Buddhists. These Buddhists lived in Bihars as Bhikshus, some were Shravakas living in Bihars, others were Tantrik Acharyas and the rest were householders. Shankara found that the Bhikshus and Shravakas were not clever to be able to argue with him but some householder Buddhist Acharyas prepared to argue with him. They brought a jar of water in which they invoked the goddess of speech Saraswati to guide them. While contending with them, Shankaracharya somehow became aware that Saraswati was invoked by his opponents therefore he entered the temple at the southern door and dismissed her after which the Buddhists became defeated. Some of them fled and some were put to death. Others who would not accept their defeat were also killed therefore many confessed that they were defeated though in reality they were not convinced that they were in error. These types of persons were ordered to sacrifice animals in direct opposition to Buddhism. Bhikshunis who were also compelled to marry householders were forced to shave the knot of hair on the crown of their heads when performing Chuda Karna thus placing the ascetics and householders on the same level. Shankara also stopped many of their religious ceremonies and cut their Brahmanical threads. There were at that time 84,000 Buddhist works which Shankara searched for and destroyed.

Shankara then went to Manichuda mountain to destroy Buddhists living there. Six times the Goddess Mani Jogini raised storms and prevented his ascending the mountain but the seventh time he succeeded. He then decided that Mahakala who was a Buddha and abhorred Himsa, should have animals sacrificed to him. Mani Jogini or Ugra Tarini was named by him Bajra Jogini. Having thus overcome the Buddhists, he introduced the Shaiva religion in the place of Buddhism. Thus ends Shankaracharya's triumph over the Buddhists of Nepal.

King Brikhadeva's brother Balarchana Deva, who was in charge of the king's pregnant wife Balarchana being uncertain whether the issue would be a son or a daughter remained at Lagankhel Ashoka chaitya and worshipped Dharmaraja Lokeshwara whose image had been consecrated by Brikhadeva, though he was desirous of living as a Bhikshu. The Queen had given birth to a son Shankaracharya caught Balarchana but the latter refused to be converted. But he was forcefully shaved and the thread was taken away from. Thus in mockery he was made a perfect Bhikshu and was forced to marry a Bhikshuni (Wright, p. 80).

But Shankaracharya was obliged to leave Buddhists in some places as priests of some temples where he found that no other persons would be able to propitiate the gods placed in them by great Buddhists. In result very few Buddhists were left in Nepal and the Bhikshus began to intermarry with the householders

(Wright, pp. 80-81).

Shankaracharya's Successor Visits Kathmandu

The genealogical work again records the coming of the Great Shankaracharya's incarnation. According to the said source (Wright, pp. 102-103) during King Bara Deva's reign a Brahman incarnation of Shankaracharya came to see whether the rules and customs established by that great reformer were still in force in Nepal. He found them observed everywhere, even at the place where Matsyendranatha by Bandhu Datta's orders. The Brahman incarnate then went to Pingala Bahal, where he found that the Bandya Acharya's hand acquired great influence by reciting mantras and worshipping Agama. After eating their meals they used to throw the remainder into the enclosure around Pashupati. Seeing this, he determined to destroy such impious people. He therefore entered into their service, and one day, when throwing away the remnants of their meal, he also threw away their Mrigathucha (a small golden bull supposed to supply the food). The next morning the Bandyas came as usual for their meal, but found no food and no Mrigathucha. They said that this was a great sin which had been committed, and therefore, they went to live elsewhere.

The Brahman then went towards Tibet, and arrived at Khasa. The Lama of Tibet, knowing that such an incarnate man had arrived, came in the disguise of a poor Tibetan, and while the Brahman was bathing, relieved the calls of nature before him. There upon the Brahman used bad language towards him, calling him Asur and a chandal. The Lama then ripped open his stomach with a knife, and asked the Brahman to do the same, so as to see which of them was purest internally. The Brahman, being afraid, transformed into a kite flew away, but the Lama transfixed him to the ground by piercing his shadow with a spear. The Lama then placed a stone on him, and performed meditation over him. The spot where this event occurred is still pointed out, where Khasa Khola is crossed. At this time a son was born to Bara Deva, who attributed this happy event to the advent of the Brahman, whom he considered to be Shankaracharya himself, after he had heard the history of that great reformer. He therefore named his son Shankara Deva in honour of Shankaracharya.

Shantikara

In Dwapara Yuga Kashyapa Buddha of Benares had came to visit the Swayambhu and Guhyeshwari shrines. From here he went to Gauda country or Bengal to suggest Prachanda Deva to go to Swayambhu and become a disciples of Gunakara Bhikshu a follower of Manjushri. Following those instructions King Prachanda Deva abdicated in favour of his son Shakti Deva and came to Nepal to live like a beggar under the name of Shantikara. The genealogical work further relates (Wright, p. 55) that later he became an authority of scriptures (Acharya) and changed his name to Shanta Shri. Afterwards he covered the Swayambhu light with stone and built a chaitya and temple over it. He also built five rooms around the Swayambhu Chaitya named Basupura, Agnipura, Bayupura, Nagapura and Shantipura in the last of which he lived in devout meditation.

The genealogy also refers later that King Prachanda Deva's son Shakti Deva's descendants had come to Nepal to find a ruling dynasty here. King Gunakama Deva is said to be of this dynasty (Wright, p. 56).

A legend is recorded in the genealogy about the drought and famine during King Gunakama Deva's rule (Wright, p. 56). With Shantikara Acharya's help the King had brought the nine Nagas under his control and caused them to give a plentiful rain and thus the drought and famine vanished.

Shantikara Acharya

Swayambhu Purana gives much importance to one Shantikara Acharya to have built the various Puras (like Shantipura) at Swayambhu Stupa. He is described as Prachanda a King of Gauda country.

He is also taken as the great Buddhist scholar Shanta Rakshita.

Shantipura

Shantikara Acharya, a former King of Bengal, had come to Swayambhu in the beginning of the Kali Yuga (Wright, p. 55). He built a stone chaitya and a temple over the Swayambhu light and five rooms around it named Basupura, Agnipura, Bayupura, Nagpura and Shantipura. In the last named room he lived absorbed in devout meditation.

In A.D. 1799 Queen Kantavati had donated a perpetual grant of 224 Muri of land of Shantipur at Swayambhu to offer worship on the Magh Purnima and Kartik Purnima day. A copper plate sheds light on this matter (D.V. Bajracharya, Shahakalka Abhilekh, Pt. 1, pp. 293-295).

Shikhi Buddha

When the Shikhi Buddha of Arun Puri city heard that the Swayambhu light had appeared on the lotus in Naga Hrada lake he came to observe and meditate on it. He also uttered several prophecies and incorporated him with the light on the Vaishakha Sankranti day (when the sun enters Aries). After this event the mountain top from where Shikhi Buddha had meditated on the Swayambhu light was called Dhyanochcha mountain. The meritorious event is commemorated by observing a Mela or fair at that place on the Mesh Sanskranti day (Wright, p. 50).

Shivadeva, King

One King Shiva Deva is described in the genealogy to have come into contact with one mendicant who was an incarnation of Durbasa. The mendicant had told the king that only path of salvation was Buddhism in this age. Therefore the king became a Buddhist Bhikshu as advised by a Buddhist teacher. He built a Bihar to live in and placed images of Swayambhu and Shakyasimha Buddha. But only four days after the king turned Bhikshu went to his teacher to report that it was impossible to him to live the life of a Bhikshu (Wright, pp. 86-87). The teacher presented evidences frcm scriptures to state that a Bhikshu can return to a married life and be called as Bajradhrik or Bajracharya. The teacher also added that people who are descendants of Shakya Muni, are after the ten Samskaras or ceremonies, Bandyas or Bhikshus, and they can also worship Kulisheshwara, and still lead a householder's life. Then the teacher took off the ochredyed cloth from the king's body, and performed the ceremony of Acharya abhisheka. Then the king built a Bihar near his own and lodged the teacher in it. Some land was assigned for his maintenance which up to the present time is given only to those who live there as Bhikshus in the Bihar called as Shivadeva Bihar,in Patan.

King Shivadeva then installed an image of Agama Devata or Buddha in his own Bihar and worshipped it. He married again and many issues were born to him.

At last while he was meditating of Lord Buddha his skull burst and his soul escaped, and obtained salvation. A mani or jewel came out of the king's skull. Only one person at a time is allowed to enter the Agama test. If more enter together, they should begin to discuss among themselves the size and shape of that jewel.

Punya Deva Varma born to Shivadeva from the wife whom he had married after becoming Bajracharya, performed his father's funeral rites and led the life of Bajracharya.

Shyamarpa Lama

The genealogical work records Shyamarpa Lama coming from Bhot (Tibet) and renewing the Garbhakath (the wooden staff round which the mound is built) of the Swayambhu Stupa and gilt the image of the deities. According to the source the event occurred in NS. 760 (A.D. 1640). The date and the name of King Lakshmi Narasimha are inscribed under the arch of the southern side of the Stupa (Wright, p. 146).

Shyamarpa Lama Repairs Swayambhu Stupa

A large stone inscription stands at the Swayambhu courtyard which is bilingual: Newari and Tibetan. It is dated NS. 878 (A.D. 1758) (D.R.

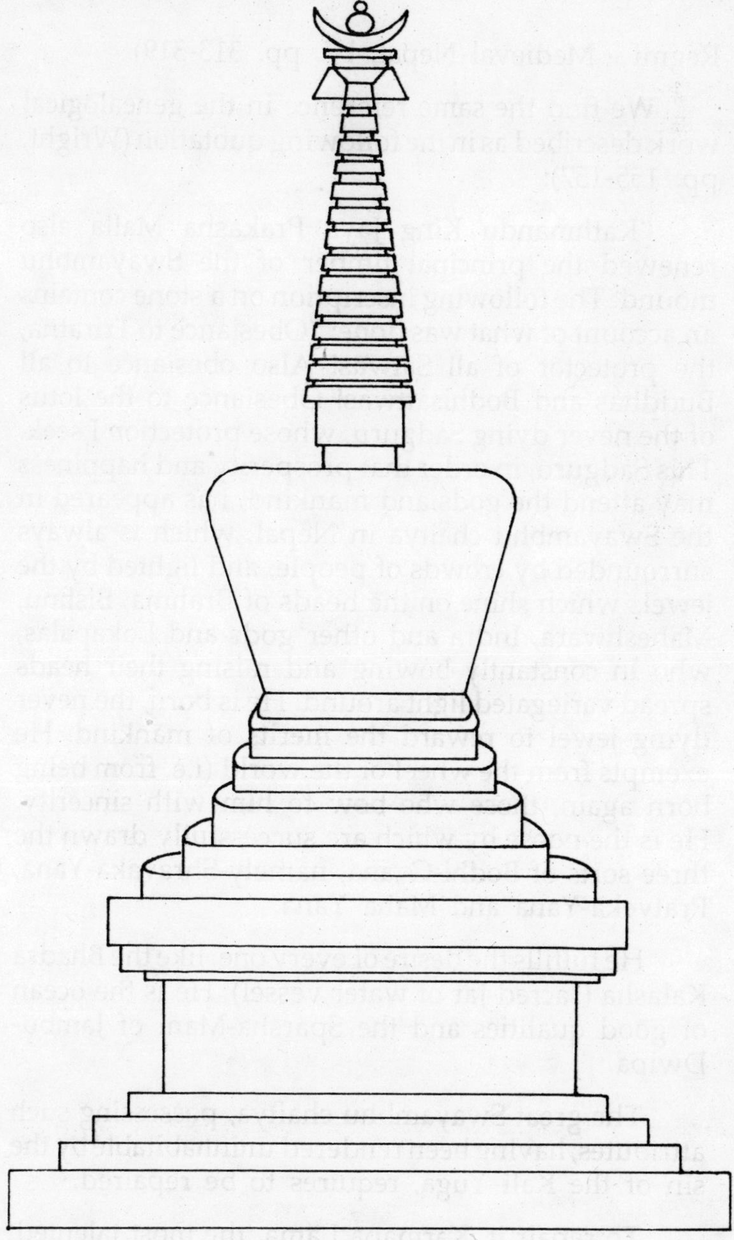

The type of Stupa built for Buddha's health by his pupils, according to Tibetan tradition

Regmi - Medieval Nepal, IV. pp. 313-319).

We find the same reference in the genealogical work described as in the following quotation (Wright, pp. 155-157):

"Kathmandu King Jaya Prakasha Malla also renewed the principal timber of the Swayambhu mound. The following inscription on a stone contains an account of what was done: "Obesiance to Triratna, the protector of all Satwas! Also obesiance to all Buddhas and Bodhisattwas! Obesiance to the lotus of the never dying Sadguru, whose protection I seek. This Sadguru, in order that prosperity and happiness may attend the gods and mankind, has appeared in the Swayambhu chaitya in Nepal, which is always surrounded by crowds of people, and lighted by the jewels which shine on the heads of Brahma, Bishnu, Maheshwara, Indra and other gods and Lokapalas, who in constantly bowing and raising their heads spread variegated light around. He is born, the never dying jewel to reward the merits of mankind. He exempts from the wheel of the world (i.e. from being born again, those who bow to him with sincerity. He is the noose by which are successfully drawn the three sorts of Bodhi-Gyana, namely-Shravaka-Yana, Pratyeka-Yana and Maha Yana.

He fulfills the desire of every one, like the Bhadra Kalasha (sacred Jar of water vessel). He is the ocean of good qualities and the Sparsha-Mani of Jambu-Dwipa.

The great Swayambhu chaitya, possessing such attributes, having been rendered uninhabitable by the sin of the Kali Yuga, requires to be repaired.

To repair it, Karmapa Lama, the most talented,

the jewel of men of arts and sciences, having a mind as clear and enlightened as the sun and moon, came from the north, in order to give happiness to the king, Kajis and people.

In N.S. 871 (A.D. 1751) in the year (of the Jupiter cycle) named Prajapati, by the Bhotiya's Keda, and by the Chinese Simu-u, he commenced the work, on an auspicious day, at a place between the Himalayas and Bindhyachala mountains. At the moment that the repairs were begun, Maha Deva, Ganapati (Ganesha) and Kumar appeared in their true forms, and said that the charge of procuring the gold and other things requisite for the work belonged to them, and that they would provide them.

Bishnu, in the form of a Brahman, came and described the kind of beam which would be required. Through the interest taken in its completion by such great gods, Shri Shri Jayaprakasha promised to carry out repairs, and the Raja of Gorkha, Shri Shri Prithwinarayana promised to have the large beam dragged to its place.

A war having broken out between the Mayurats country and Lahor, and it being necessary to conclude a treaty between Bhot and Nepal, the Lama was obliged to return to his own country. On arriving at Keron, he said that he would not be able to return to Nepal, but that one of the five Karmapa Lamas would come in his place and be as good as himself. If this could not be arranged, a disciple of his would come, whom the people should trust and through him complete repairs. He then returned to Bhot.

Then came Brug-Pa-Chikhyempa, the omniscient, the disciple of the former Lama, who, assisted by Shakya Bhikshu and Shasanadhara, completed the repairs according to the directions of Karmapa Lama, suffering great hardships. It was completed in N.S. 878 (A.D. 1758), and was consecrated by Brug-Pa-Thyang-Chikyem-Pa and Bira Ratna Lamas.

Account of expenditure 1382 Dharnis of copper, 2045 tolas of gold. The whole gold expended on it was 3344 tolas and ten mashas. Shahi rupees 4775, one Dharni one seer and 2 paos of silver. Two Dharnis of pure gold. Charit Mohars 14106. If all the Khatas, Kochin (kinds of silk), tea, ghi, salt, oil and flesh, be taken into account, the total cost comes to 43,639 rupees, besides 67 horses and 21 pieces of Kochin. The musk used in applying to the deity was worth 1000 rupees.

May the temple extend protection to every living creature. The inscription on this stone was formerly cut an another one but Karmapa Lama, coming on a pilgrimage to Akshobhya Buddha at Swayambhu, saw the stone broken and took it to Bhot, and this one is a copy of the former one.

May the King, Kajis, and every living creatures of this country obtain salvation, and be endowed with the title of Samyak Buddha by being absorbed into Shri Shri Shri Bajradhara Bajrasattwa Satchit Buddha" (Wright, pp. 155-157).

Simha Sarthabahu

The main deity of the Thama Bahil or Bikramashila Bihar which is a peculiar instance because the Biharas generally enshrine Buddha or other deities. A legend is also recorded in the genealogical work relating to Simha Sarthabahu and the Bihara.

Stupa, Thahiti

A Stupa was built after covering a water conduit (called Suvarma Pranali, which gave name to the Kathmandu City Suvarna Pranali Mahanagara) during Patra Mahendraraja's chieftainship in A.D. 1432. Later during King Surya Malla's rule it was renovated in A.D. 1524 (see M. Slusser, *Nepala Mandala*, p. 90).

Sudhanwa, King

With Manju Pattan city's King Sudhanwa, a descendant of King Dharmapal, the Treta Yuga is said to have ended. The genealogy states that this king became displeased with his capital city of Manju Pattan and therefore changed his capital (Wright, p. 54). He built a town on the banks of Ikshumati (Tukucha) which he named Sankashya Nagari. The king is also said to have participated in King Janaka's arrangement for Sita's Swayamvara at Janakpur. But King Janaka had killed Sudhanwa to appoint his own brother Kushadhwaja as king of the Sankashya Nagari.

Sunaya Shri Mishra

The genealogy has retained a legend relating to a Sunaya Shri Mishra Brahman of Kapilbastu who had gone to Lhasa to achieve spiritual guidance (Wright, p. 77). In Lhasa he met a Lama who possessed the power of flying in the air, of hearing sounds from the distance of thousands of miles, of seeing for thousands of miles, the knowledge of what is in the minds of others, the knowing of all past events, freedom from sensual and worldly desires. He could live and die at his own will. Rebirth was under his power. He could also tell the events of present, past and future times. All these powers were acquired by him by performing penances according to Lord Buddha's preachings. After being instructed on spiritual matters by such a Lama Sunaya Shri Mishra returned to Kathmandu to find there a building for Bihar. First he could not select a spot to fix his abode but finally he selected at one of the four Ashoka chaityas built by Ashoka. He presented a crystal jewel to King Rudra Deva Varma to have a piece of ground to fix his abode. Since he was directed he put a crystal jewel in one of the great Ashoka chaityas and repaired all four. His two disciples of Kapilbastu Govardhana Mishra and Kashyapa Mishra were also made to settle at two Bihars named Danta Bihar and Lahbana Bihar.

When Sunaya Shri Mishra's mother (wife?) and sons came to inquire about him they were also got settled in a house near the former's Bihar. When a grandson was born he made his son become a mendicant and this was made a rule for the succeeding generations also.

The Bihara built by Sunaya Shri Mishra is now called Yampi Bihar. His disciples lived at Konti Bahi Bihar and Pintha Bihar.

Surat Bajra and His Lhasa Visit

During Kathmandu King Shiva Simha Malla's reign one Buddhist powerful Tantrik Surat Bajra is said in the genealogy to have gone to Lhasa. This journey was considered a difficult undertaking. One day he was taking tea with the Lama of Tibet, he saw his house on fire, and succeeded in extinguishing the flames by throwing tea on them (Wright, p. 142).

Taudaha

The genealogical work states that when Manjushri Bodhisattwa had cut through the mountain to let the water run out the Naga King living here was also going outside. But the Bodhisattwa persuaded the Naga King Karkotaka to remain and on Mesha Sankranti day (Vaishakha Sankranti) he appointed him to live in a lake called Taudaha (the big lake) (Wright, p. 51).

Thakuri Rulers and Buddhism

The local rulers of Kathmandu, the Thakuris are said to have built numerous Buddhist temples, with lands assigned for their maintenance in Patan, Kathmandu and Bhaktapur during their 225 year rule (Wright, pp. 116-117).

Thamel

King Gunakama Deva had founded a village named Thama Bahil, at the place where formerly Bikramashila Bihar stood. The image of Thama Bahil, consecrated by Simhal Baniya, had been destroyed when the waters of the Bagmati had been stopped by Danasur, but it had been replaced by the descendants of Simhal (Wright, p. 104).

Tibet and Nepal Exchange Buddhist Cultures

The two countries are separated by the Himalayas which is generally inaccessible in all weathers. But the nature has been kind enough to allow to have some passes through the Himalayas so that the two continents could come more closer politically and culturally.

There are at least 18 pass areas between Nepal and Tibet of which only two are used for extensive commercial purposes i.e. Kuti and Kerung.

All the passes are at elevations from 15000 to 20000 feet above sea level and are closed throughout the winter months.

Tirtha Bihara

One ancient King Narendra Deva is described in the genealogy to have built a Bihar near the temple of Lumadi Bhadrakali named it Tirtha Bihar and gave it to Bandhu Datta Bajracharya (Wright, p. 93). King Narendra Deva had put his second son Ratna Deva under Bandhu Datta's guidance in Tirtha Bihar.

Bandhu Datta had placed Padmantaka Bhairava, ten Krodha Devatas (attending deities) from Kamuni in the Tirtha Bihar. At the north-east corner of the Tirtha Bihar he placed Mahakala brought from Tibet. Licchavi King Gunakama Deva III is also said to have built the Sankata Bhairav Temple at Te Bahal (or Tirtha Vihar).

The Bihar is also called as Tairatha Bihar (Wright, p. 94).

Types of Buddhist Bhikshus

Among Buddhist Newars the Bhikshus are divided into 5 categories:

1. Vajracharya or Gurubhaju
2. Shakya Bhikshu or Bandeju
3. Shramanera or Shramani Bandeju
4. Brahmacharya Bhikhu or Bhikhu Bandeju
5. Chailaka Bhikhu (Chivaha Bandeju)

Vaitaragas

Swayambhu Purana gives Buddhist identical names to the following 8 famous Shivalingas (Phallic emblem of Shiva) (Ashakazi Bajracharya - Nepala Tirtha Vrata Pustakam, pp. 14-16):

	Buddhist Name	Shaivite Name
1.	Maitri Bodhisattwa	Mani Lingeshvara of Manichuda Lake
2.	Gaganaganj Bodhisattwa	Gokarneshvara
3.	Samanta Bhadra Bodhisattwa	Kileshvaraof Changu
4.	Vajrapani Bodhisattwa	Kumbheshvara of Patan
5.	Manjughosh Bodhisattwa	Gopaleshvara of Pharping
6.	Sarvani Varma Viskumbhi Bodhisattwa	Phanikeshvara of Pharping
7.	Kshitigarbha Bodhisattwa	Gandeshvara or Garteshvara of Chobhar
8.	Khagarva Bodhisattwa	Bikrameshvara or Adeshvara of Phasku

Yamaleshwara Lokeshwara

It is mentioned in the genealogical work that during King Yaksha Malla's reign some potters, while digging for clay, found an image of Lokeshwara, which had been made by Gunakama Deva Raja, but which had been buried under the ruins of the temple that fell down during the period of the Thakuri Rajas. The Raja Yaksha Malla got the image repaired and got it into a new temple, which he built for it in Kathmandu. The image henceforth was named Yamaleshwara, and the place where it was dug up was called Yamala or Jamala (Wright, pp. 128-129).

Yogambar Janana Shri

The shrine of Mhaipi Ajima is worshipped by Newar Buddhists calling 'Yogambar Janana Shri' (Dhana Shamsher Rana, Kamakala Rahasya, T.U. 2036, p. 101).

Yoga Narendra Malla's Attitude Towards Buddhism

Patan King Yoga Narendra Malla is reported in the genealogical work to have given a copy of the text of Karanda Byuha, containing the history of Matsyendra Natha, written in golden letters, to Dharmaraja Pandit of Onkuli Bihar, who recited this Purana in Manimandapa. The Pandit gave the following benediction to the Raja —" O Raja Yoga Narendra, may the Loka Natha, who had vanquished the wicked and made the people go in the right path, protect thee! O Raja, the history contained in the books which thou hast given to me, has been recited to the people, and shall be recited again and again. For this meritorious act may happiness attend thee, and mayest thou live long with good health, and reign over the people (Wright, p. 169).

Appendix

Kapilbastu in the Buddhist Books by T. Watters[1]

The recent discoveries in Nepal associated with the name of Dr. Fûhrer, Archaeological Surveyor in the

---

[1] from Journal of Royal Asiatic Society, 1898, pp. 533-571.

employment of the Government of India, may lead at an early date to a revival of interest in the life of the historical Buddha, distinguished generally by the names Gautama and Sakyamuni, and in the district in which he is supposed to have been born.

The first of these discoveries was an Ashoka pillar, found in 1893 near the tank of Nigliva, a village in the Nepalese Terai (or Tarai), about 37 miles to the north-west of the Usha station of the North Bengal Railway. This pillar has an inscription which records that King Asoka, fourteen years after he had ascended the throne, personally worshipped the *tope* of the Buddha Konakamana, and added to it for the second time. From the travels of the Chinese pilgrims Fa-hsien and Yuan-chuang[2] we learn to some extent how this *tope* stood with respect to the site of Kapilavastu, visited by them. Then last year the official explorers discovered in the same district another Asokà pillar, also bearing an inscription. In this second inscription the king states that he set up this pillar in the Lumbini village (presumed to be not far from Kapilavastu) at the very spot where Sakyamuni Buddha was born. Further investigations, we are informed, are to be made in this interesting district, and these may lead to more discoveries of still greater importance. The ruins in the neighbourhood are said to be very extensive, and it is not unlikely that among them some more old inscriptions may be found.

While waiting for the results of future explorations, however, we may find it profitable to make a review of the information we have about the city and district of

---

2 The common ways of writing the names of these pilgrims are Fa-hien and Hiouen-Thsang; they are also written Fa Hien (or Hian) and Hiuen Tsiang. In Chinese the name of the former is written and that of the latter (also)

Kapilavastu, and the connection of Gautama Buddha therewith. This information, unfortunately, is for the most part of a most unsatisfactory nature, being chiefly to be found in legends and romances, about which it is impossible to determine whether they are in any degree based on facts, and in narratives partly derived from the romances or other questionable sources. These narratives are to be found in the various editions of the Vinaya, and in other canonical works. There are also incidental notices to be found in these treatises of Buddha's visits to various towns and cities, and of his travels as a religious teacher. It is not to be supposed, however, that all these notices and records are to be regarded as authentic narratives of facts. They were probably believed to be true by the hearers and the narrators, but we have no means of deciding when they are and when they are not correct information.

The statements and opinions given in the following pages are mainly derived from Buddhist books in Chinese translations. These books are of very unequal value, and they often vary to a remarkable degree in their descriptive and narrative passages. It often seems to be impossible to reconcile their conflicting statements, or to regard them as being derived from a common original. No attempt can be made here to account for these discrepancies, or to estimate the correct value of the testimony of the various authorities. Our task is simply to try and find out what these scriptures tell us about the town and district of Kapilavastu in the lifetime of Gautama Buddha, and his connection with them.

The periods about which the few Pali and Sanskrit books quoted in the following pages were composed may be regarded as tolerably well known. For the works which are to be found only in Tibetan and

Chinese translations we have only the dates of the translations with occasional scraps of information as external evidence, and in a few cases the probable period of the composition is indicated by the contents. Such popular books as Hardy's "Manual of Buddhism, " Foucaux's "Rgya Tcher Rol Pa," and Mr. Beal's "Romantic History" are supposed to be familiar to the reader, and little reference is made to them here. The works principally used as authorities are Chinese translations of Buddhist books not generally accessible, and belonging largely to the Vinaya and Agama compilations on one hand, and to the group of Romances on the other.[3]

Origin and Supposed Site of Kapilavastu

The legends and romances about the great religious reformer of India known as Gautama Buddha describe him as having been born in the Lumbini Garden, near the city of Kapilvastu. This city, according to the mythical accounts of the Buddha's royal ancestors, had been founded by the sons of an Ikshvaku king of the Solar race. The king, who reigned at Potalaka according to some or at Saket according to others, yielding to the intrigues of his queen or concubine, drove his four sons into exile. These princes, accompanied by their sisters and a large retinue, went northwards, and after a long journey halted at a pleasant suitable site near the hermitage of a rishi named Kapila. The rishi welcomed the exiles, and with solemn rite gave over to them a piece of ground on which to settle and build their city. When the city was laid out

[3] The texts used are those of the recent Japanese revised edition of the collection of Buddhist books kept in the libraries of the monasteries in China, Japan, and Korea. References are given, however, to Mr. Bunyio Nanjio's valuable Catalogue, and the dates of the transalations are taken from that work.

and occupied, the settlers called it in gratitude Kapilavastu or Kapilanagara, from the name of their kind patron. This happened in a period of remote antiquity.

The city of Kapilavastu thus found was, according to the generally received accounts, situated near or at the southern slopes of the Himavan mountains, and in the kingdom of Kosala. It was on the banks of a river, it had a lake (or pond), and it was on the borders of a copse of saka or teak trees. In the Chinese translations the river on which the city stood is called Bhagira or Bhagirathi or Ganges, and the name Rohini for it does not seem to occur[4].

It must be noticed, however, that in some of the Chinese texts the site of Kapilavastu is placed in a district to the north of the Himavan, the royal exiles being represented as having crossed this range and settled on the south side of a mountain beyond. Thus, according to one version of the story, Siddhartha (the Buddha), replying to King Bimbisara's questions about his home and family, says: "I was born to the north of the Snow Mountains in the Sakka country, in the city of Kapilavastu; my father's name is Suddhodana, and the family name is Gautama[5]. This conflict of authorities as to whether Kapilavastu was to the south or the north of the Himavat mountains is interesting in connection with circumstances to be related hereafter. But the

---

4 Fo-pen-hsing-chi-ching, ch. 4 (Bunyio Nanjio's Catalogue, No. 680, tr. 587), here quoted by the short title "Hsing-chi-ching." Bunyio Nanjio's Catalogue is quoted by the abbreviation "Bun".

5 Mi-sha-sai-ho-hai-wu-fen-lii, ch. 15 (Bun., No. 1,222, tr. 424), here quoted by its usual short title "Wu-ten Vinaya"; Ssu-fen-lu-tsang, ch. 31 (Bun., No. 1,117, tr. 405), here quoted by the short title "Ssu-fen-Vinaya."

majority of texts is in favour of the supposition that the city was situated on or near the southern slopes of these mountains.

Accepting this theory, however, when we try to learn from the Buddhist scriptures the precise situation of Kapilavastu with respect to other towns and cities, we are rather disappointed. We are told, for example, that it was in the centre of the world or of Jambudvipa[6], a description very unsatisfactory from the geographical point of view. More precise statements place the city not in Kosala but in the Vrijjian country, and the "Chang-a-han-ching" makes it to have been situated not far from Pava, a considerable town of that country[7]. These statements are of importance, as we shall see at a subsequent stage. From Sravasti, the capital of Kosala, to Kapilavastu was a journey of three days for Suddodana's messenger, but one of seven days and nights for the wretched old king Prasenajit and his queen when fugitives[8]. From the two Chinese pilgrims Fa-hsien and Yuan-chuang (Hiouen Thsang) we learn that the Kapilavastu which they visited was about ninety miles distant from Sravasti in a south-east direction[9].From Rajagriha to Kapilavastu the distance was, according to the "Jataka," sixty yojanas, and according to some other authorities fifty yojanas, the

---

6 I-cu-u-p'u-sa-pen-ch-i-ching, p. 2 (Bun., No. 509, tr. about 314); Hsiu-hsing-pen-ch'i-ching, ch.1(Bun., No. 664, tr. 197), the "Charya-nidana-sutra."

7 Chang-a-han-ching, ch. 12 (Bun., No. 545, tr. 413).

8 Ken-pen-shuo-i-ch'ie-yu-pu-p'i-na-ye, P'o-seng-shi, ch. 9 (Bun.,No. 1,123, tr. 710). This and the other portions of the Vinaya of the Sarvastivadin School are here quoted by the short title "Sarvata Vinaya," with the title of each section added. Liu-li-wang-ching (Bun., No. 671, tr. about 300).

9 Fo-kuo-chi, ch. 22; Hsi-yu-chi, ch. 6.

Amogha Siddha

"Hsing-chi-ching" placing the former city to the south of the latter[10]. In the "Sutta Nipata" certain Brahmins setting out from the neighbourhood of Alaka in the Deccan, made a pilgrimage to Buddha at Sravasti (Savatti) and back. There route lay by Ujjeni and other places to Kosambi and Saket, thence on to Savatthi, Setavyam, Kapilavastu, and Kusinara, and round to Pava and Vaishali, the Magadhan city, and the Stone Chaitya[11]. Dr. Oldenberg is evidently satisfied with the simple enumeration of places in this passage, but it cannot be said to add much to our knowledge and it is apparently second hand.

It is not necessary here to refer at length to the identification of the site of Kapilavastu made by Mr. Carlaeyl and accepted by General Cunningham. The discovery of the Asoka pillars in the neighbourhood of Nigliva shows us that the Kapilavastu of Asoka and the Chinese pilgrims was in that district. "Nigliva is a small Napalese village in the Tarai, or lowland below the hills, in the Tahsil Taulehva of Zilla Butwal, about thirty-eight miles north-west of the Uska Bazar station on the Bengal and North-Western Railway." Paderia, the site of the Lumbini Garden, is about two miles north of the town of Bhagvanpur in the same district. Here, we are told, are the ruins of Kapilvastu covering an immense space, "to be traced over a length of seven English miles and a breadth of about three English miles.[12]

---

[10] Jataka (ed. Fausboll), vol. i, p. 87; Hsing-chi-ching, chs. 23, 37; Ching-fan-wang-pan-nie-p'an-ching (Bun., No. 732, tr. 455).

[11] Sutta Nipata, p. 184 (P.T.S.); Oldenberg's "Buddha, "S. 110 (3rd edition).

[12] "The Birthplace of Gautama Buddha," by V.A. Smith, in Journal R.A.S., July, 1897, p. 616; Buhler, in Sitz. K.A. d. Wiss. in Wien, Phil. hist., January 7, 1897).

We should remember, however, that Kapilavastu is not represented in all the Buddhist scriptures as the large and floourshing city endowed with many monasteries and other public buildings. In most of the romances and in the descriptions taken from or founded on these, it is generally a great and glorious city with the magnificence of a royal capital. But in several treatises it is also represented as a small unimportant town without any attractions. According to a legend given in the "Sarvata Vanaya" it was insufficient for the wants of the young Sakya colonists even at a very early period of their history. In that work we read that when the families of the Ikshvaku princes were growing up Kapila complained that their noise disturbed his religious exercises. He proposed to go away, but the Sakyas persuaded him to remain, and he assigned them a good site at a short distance from his hermitage. Here the city was built to which Kapila's name was given, and it was occupied by the families of the exiles. But this city was soon found to be too small, and the families had to remove to another place, where under the guidance of a deva they settled and built a new city, which they called Devadaha. This is the Kola and Vyaghrapattha (or Vyaghrapur) of various treatises, and a different origin for it is given in several other legends. Again, in certain Abhidharma treatises, such as the "Tachih-tu-lun," we find Kapilavastu referred to as a small town inferior to Sravasti, and in some enumerations of the great cities of "Central India" its name does not appear.[13] It is true, however, that Ananda is made to describe it as a beautiful and splendid city.

As we have seen, some Chinese translations of Buddhist texts put Kapilavastu far north beyond the

---

[13] Sarvat Vinaya, P'o-send-shi, ch. 2; Ta-chin-tu-lun, ch. 3 (Bun., No. 1,169, tr. 405).

Snow Mountains (the Himavan or Himalayas). This fact helps to explain some extraordinary statements to be found in other Chinese books. Thus the Life of the pilgrim Chih-meng places Kapilavastu 1,300 li (about 260 miles) to the south-west of a place called K'i-sha, that is, perhaps, Gesh. In this latter country the pilgrim saw the Buddha's bowl and marble spittoon, and at Kapilavastu he saw a hair and a tooth of the Buddha, his ushnisha, and his luminous image in the rock. The pilgrim Chih-meng was in India about the year 435 A.D. Then the Life of Buddhabhadra, a contemporary of Fa-hsien, describes that man, doubtless on his own testimony, as a Sakka, a man of Kapilavastu, and a descendant of Prince Amritodana. But this man is also described as having been born at the city of Na-k'o-li in North India. In these two narratives Kapilavastu seems to be identified or confounded with Nagar, a once famous place in the Jellalabad Valley, wrongly identified with the Nagarahara of a later Chinese traveller.[14]

For the names Kapila and Kapilavastu the Chinese seem to have obtained from their foreign teachers several explanations more or less correct. Thus we find Ts'ang-se or 'Azure-colour' given as the meaning of Kapila. This term 'Azure-colour' was also applied to the appearance of Siddhartha's face at the end of his long period of fasting and self-mortification, and in each case it is expressive of the man's sallow, starved appearance. But Kapila is better translated by Huang-fa, or Yellow-Hair, or by Huang-t'ou, Yellow-Head, and the city is Huang-t'ou-chu, as if Kapilavastu, the residence of Kapila. Another interpretation of the name of the city is Miao-te, Excellent-virtue or Fine-qualities. Then the Kapilavastu district or the Sakka

[14] Kao-seng-chuan, chs. 2, 3.

region is mentioned by the name Chih-tse-kuo, or Redmarshcountry, evidently the translation of a Sanskrit term. In connection with this last name it may be mentioned that in the year A.D.428 an embassy from Yue-ai, Moon-loved, king of the Ka-p'i-li country, arrived in China. This country—that is, its capital—was described as situated on the side of a lake to the east of a river, and surrounded on all sides by dark purplish rocks. Ka-p'i-li may be for Kapilavastu, or it may be for some other district in India, but it could not have been the Kapilavastu visited by Fa-hsien.[15]

Kapilavastu as Seen and Described by Asoka and the Chinese Pilgrims

As is well known, the great King Asoka is represented as having made a personal visit, under the guidance of the venerable Sthavira Upagupta, to Kapilavastu and the Lumbini Garden.[16] Several centuries after his time these places were visited by the Chinese pilgrim Fa-hsien, and two centuries later by another Chinese pilgrim, Yuan-chuang (Hiouen Thsang).

It may be useful for us to recall here the various objects of Buddhistic interest at Kapilavastu as enumerated in the "Asokavadana" and in the narratives of the above-mentioned Chinese pilgrims. Fa-hsien describes the city as a wilderness, with no inhabitants beyond the congregation of Buddhist monks and a score or two of lay people, and all the country round as in a similar state of utter desolation. The second pilgrim

---

15 Sung shu, ch. 57. The name of this country, Ka-p'i-li, occurs also in other Chinese treatises, and it was evidently not Kapilavastu.

16 Divyavadana, p. 390 ff.; A-yu-wang-chuan (Bun., No. 1,459, tr. about 300); A-yu-wang-ching (Bun., No. 1,343, tr. 512).

found all the towns of the district in the same deserted condition, but he mentions the foundations of the walls of the city as still visible. For his information about these foundations the pilgrim was undoubtedly indebted to the local monks and all the various sites were evidently known only by the memorials which had been erected on them.

At Kapilavastu on the site of Suddhodana's palace Fa-hsien saw a representation of the Prince's (i.e. the Buddha's) mother with the Prince about to enter her womb on a white elephant. This was apparently seen by Yuan-chauang also, who mentions another likeness (or image) of the queen and one of the king. Further, Fa-hsien saw topes (or chaityas rather) on the spots where the Prince outside the east gate of the city saw the sick man and told his coachman to drive back, and, it is to be inferred, outside the other gates where the old man, the corpse, and the religious ascetic were seen. These are also mentioned by Yuan-chuang, but Upagupta only pointed out to Asoka the place where Siddhartha, oppressed by the thoughts of old age, sickness, and death, went away to the forest. The two Chinese pilgrims saw the memorial at the place where Asita predicted the infant Prince's future, and this spot was also pointed out to Asoka. The pilgrims further mention memorials at the places where the Prince, in competition with his kinsmen, shot the arrow which produced a spring of water, where the father met his son when the latter was coming to the city for the first time as Buddha, and where the 500 young Sakyas were admitted into the new Order. Fa-hsien alone mentions a tope at the place where, while the Buddha was preaching to the devas, the Four Deva-rajahs guarded the doors so that his father could not enter. Both pilgrims tell of the tope at the place where the Buddha, sitting under a banyan (or a large tree) accepted a robe from Prajapati, the banyan being seen apparently by Fa-hsien at least. This tree, according to Yuan chuang, was close to the Monastery of the Banyan Park, which he places three or four li (about two-thirds of a mile) to the south of the city. The Nyagrodharama (Nigrodharama) or Banyan Park (or Arama) was to the Buddhists one of the most interesting sights of Kapilavastu, and one cannot understand why it is not mentioned in the "Asokavadana." Here the Buddha sojourned and delivered some of his discourses, and Yuan-chuang saw in it an Asoka tope at the spot where the Buddha preached to his father. We find the place called the 'Sakyas' Arama" and the "Sakyas' Banyan-Park Vihara, " but commonly it is simply the Banyan Park (Arama). It is also called in Chinese translation the "To-ken-shu-yuan," the Park (or Arama) of the many-rooted tree. This was evidently a place of resort and temporary residence before it had a Buddhist establishment. It may be doubted whether there was any building here, at least during the time of the Buddha. We are told, indeed, of Suddhodana building a monastery here, and Yuan-chuang makes the Buddha, on the occasion of his first visit, stay in the Nigrodharama. But the Buddha is generally described as being in the arama forest sitting under a tree or under the trees. It was in the establishment here that he, as the pilgrims narrate, accepted from his devoted foster-mother the beautiful vestment which she had made for him, handing it over to the congregation of the brethren. Both pilgrims mention the topes which commemorated events in the invasion of the city and slaughter of its inhabitants by King Virudhika, and of the one which marked the place where the Prince sat under a tree (according to the "Asokavadana" a jambu) and watched the ploughers at work. Yuan-chuang

Basundhara Devi

alone mentions a temple or chaitya with a representation of the Prince on his white horse in the air, that is, in the act of flying over the city wall, also the temple to which the infant Prince was born in order to be presented to the guardian deity. This temple was pointed out also by Upagupta to Asoka, then still the shrine of the "Yaksha who gave the Sakyas increase," but in Yuan chuang's time a temple of Mahesvara. This pilgrim also tells of a chaitya with representations of Rahula and of his mother, not mentioned by Fa-hsien, and he alone tells of the Elephant Ditch and the chaitya in which the Prince was represented as a schoolboy. The site of the schoolroom was pointed out to Asoka by his guide.

Other places are mentioned in the Asoka romance which are not in the narratives of the Chinese pilgrims. These are the spot at which King Suddhodana prostrated himself in adoration of the infant Prince; the place at which the foster-mother Prajapati nursed the motherless baby; the place where the boy became accomplished in the art of riding, driving, and the use of arms and the place where, encompassed by 100,000 devas, he enjoyed himself with 60,000 pretty girls. The texts from which the Chinese translations were made do not make devas attend the Prince while he frolicked with his maidens.

Now we cannot fail to observe that all the sites mentioned in the Asoka romance, and nearly all those described in the narratives of the pilgrims, derive their existence from the romances and legends about the Buddha's birth and early life. The romances generally terminate with an account of the triumphal return of the Prince as Buddha to his native city. As to subsequent events of his lifetime, the Chinese pilgrims tell us only of memorials connected with Virudhika's invasion.

This event is not referred to in the "Asokavadana," but, as we shall presently see, it is narrated with variations of detail in several of the old Buddhist texts.

On the other hand, there were certain objects in or at Kapilvastu of which the Asoka romance and the pilgrims' narratives do not make any mention. These objects are all referred to in the Buddhist scriptures, and they were all connected with the great Master's career. Now we know that Asoka and the pilgrims travelled in India with the express purpose of personally visiting the scenes of the Buddha's life and work. So their silence as to the sites and other objects now to be mentioned is very note-worthy.

Among the places which the pilgrims might have been expected to see and describe, one of the most important was the site of the great Santhagara or Assembly Hall. This hall, about which Yuan-chuang knew, was built by the Sakyas of Kapilavastu in the Buddha's time, and it was evidently a large and solid structure with stone pavement and furnished with pillars. When it was finished the Sakyas of the city decreed that it was not to be used by anyone until it had been formally opened and used by the Buddha. The use of the hall by the young prince Virudhika before the inauguration was resented by the Sakyas as a desecration, and, according to some authorities, led ultimately to the dreadful results presently to be described. There is some doubt as to the situation of the Hall: some texts placing it inside the city, and others putting it a short distance outside.[17]

---

17 P'i-na-ye or Chie-yin-yuan-ching, ch. 4 (Bun., No. 1,130, tr. 378); Tsa-a-han-ching, ch. 43 (Bun., No. 544, tr. 420 to 479); Samyut, Nikaya, vol. iv, p. 182 (P.T.S.); I-tsu-ching, ch. 2 (Bun., No. 674, tr. 222 to 280); Tseng-i-a-han-ching, ch. 26 (Bun., No. 543, tr. 385).

Another very interesting place near the city was the "Sow's Tank." By the side of this was the "Arama of the Parivradjaka tirthikas, called the place of the Sow." Another name for this arama was the "Udumbara Arama" of the Non-Buddhists (tirthikas). It was near this that Ananda found the mangled and scattered remains of the thousands of Sakya killed with cruel torture by King Virudhika. [18]

Then there was a tope close to a banyan-tree outside that gate of the city through which the Prince passed when he went out into the wilderness to seek the way of salvation. There was also the tope erected at their city by the Sakyas of Kapilavastu over the share of the Buddha's relics which they had obtained from the Mallas of Kusinagara, and of this tope or its ruins there should have been mentioned. [19]

Further, near the Banyan Park was the Mahavana or Great Wood to which the Buddha sometimes resorted. He is represented as passing the afternoon here absorbed in religious meditation (that is, sleeping) under a bilva-tree. The Great Wood may be another name for the Kapilavat Wood, in which the Buddha sojourned once with his 500 arhats. We read also the "P'i-lo-ye-chi(ti) Clump," to which the Buddha walked from the Banyan Arama, and in which he was visited by the Dandapani of Kapilavastu. This was perhaps a clump of bilva-trees in the Great Wood.[20]

[18] Abhidharmamahavibhasha-lun, ch. 105 (Bun., No. 1,263, tr. 659); Vibhasha-lun, ch. 13 (Bun., No. 1,279, tr. 383); Rockhill, Life of the Buddha, p. 120.

[19] Hsing-chi-ching, ch. 17, Mo-ho-Mo-ye-ching, ch. 2 (Bun., No. 382, tr. about 560); Pan-ni-huan-ching, ch. 2 (Bun., No. 119, tr. about 350). In S.B.E., vol. xi, p. 134, Mr. Rhys Davids, by a slip, omits this tope, which is duly mentioned in the "Mahaparinibbana suttam" (Journal R.A.S., vol. viii, p. 260).

[20] Maj. Nakaya, vol. i, 108 (P.T.S.); Tseng-i-a-han-ching, ch. 35.

At Kapilavastu there was also the "Sakyas' vihara of the Bamboo wood," also resorted to by the Buddha for afternoon meditation. Here, too, he was visited by the Dandapani of the city, who asked him about the essentials of his teaching and went away dissatisfied with the answer. We read also of the Buddha staying it Kapilavastu in the Bihara called Ka-lo-ch'a-mo'Shi-ching-she, that is, perhaps, Kala-Kshama Sakya Vihara, the Vihara of the Black-earth Sakyas. Near this there was the "Kala Sakya Vihara, and this also was visited by the Buddha.[21] These were apparently large establishments, with accomodation for many bhikshus. Neither in the "Asokavadana" nor in the narratives of the Chinese pilgrims have we any reference to any of these interesting objects. There was also in the immediate vicinity of Kapilavastu other sites, of less importance perhaps, but hallowed by the presence of the Buddha or one or more of his great disciples. These also were apparently not pointed out to the pilgrims, and are not mentioned in their books.

Various Places in the Sakya Country

The names "Kapila Country" and "Kapilavastu" are sometimes used to denote the city proper and sometimes the city together with the district in which it was situated. But this district was only part of a large region to which the Sakyas gave their name. In this region there were, we learn, eight or ten towns in addition to Kapilavastu. We find also certain villages, rivers, parks, and religious settlements mentioned in the scriptures as having been visited by the Buddha or as in some other way connected with his life and work. The most interesting of these places is the Lumbini Garden, the scene of the Buddha's entrance on his last

[21] Chung-a-han-ching, chs. 28 and 49 (Bun., No. 542, tr. 398).

existence. This garden was in the territory of the King of Devadaha, and according to the "Hsing-chi-ching" beyond that city. But it is generally represented as on the Kapilavastu side of Devadaha, and in the "Jataka" it is expressly stated to be between the two cities and used by the inhabitants of both.[22] According to the Chinese pilgrims the garden lay about 50 li (ten miles) to the east of Kapilavastu. The name is found transcribed in Chinese in several ways, pointing to differences in original authorities. Yuan-chuang, and he along, writes La-fa-ni, i.e. Lavani, the Beautiful Woman, Fa-hsien writes Lun-min (or bin), i.e. Lumin or Lumbin. In the "A-yu-wang-chuan" we have Lin-mou-ni or Lummini, and in the "A-yu-wang-ching" and other books we have Lam-p'i-ni or Lumbini. There are several other transcriptions, but they all stand for forms like Lummini or Lumbini.

According to some legends the Garden had its name from the beautiful queen of the King of Koli (or Davadaha), the mother of the Buddha's mother. But in the "A-yu-wang-ching" the name is explained as meaning 'the place of emancipation,' and we also find the word interpreted as denoting mie, 'extinction,' or tuan, 'cut off.'

According to the recent investigations the old name still survives in the "Rumindei" of the Napalese Terai, the place in which a pillar has been discovered with an interesting inscription. From this inscription we learn that King Asoka came to the spot and worshipped at it as the place at which the Buddha Sakyamuni was born that the king set up here "a stone pillar with a stone horse on it, and reduced the land-tax on the Lummini village" because it was the birthplace of the Buddha. This is said to "set at rest all doubt as to

---

[22] Jataka, vol. i, p. 52.

the exact site of the traditional birthplace of Gautama Buddha."[23] But it would be more correct to say that the inscription, if genuine, tells us what was the spot indicated to Asoka as the birthplace of the Buddha.

Another important place was the city of the Sakyan Kolians, which had its own king or governor. This city had the names Kola (or Koli or Koti) and Devadaha and Vyaghra-pur (or -patha). The Chinese pilgrims do not seem to have known anything about this city, and they, like some other authors, regarded the Lumbini Garden as within the territory of the King of Kapilavastu. Yet the town was connected with the history of the Buddha's ancestors and his own life, and it was visited by him. Thus we read of him that "once he was staying among the Sakyas in their town called Devadaha." The distance of this town from Kapilavastu is given in one treatise as 800 li (about 160 miles), but in most of the books the distance seems to be small. Thus we find the ladies of the two cities coming with offerings of flowers to the Buddha in the Banyan Arama.[24]

Between the Koli territory and that of Kapilavastu ran the river called in the Chinese texts Luhita or Luhoka or Luhitaka, that is, Rohiti or Rohitaka, and in the Pali texts Rohini. At the time of the Buddha's residence at Kapilavastu an enormous hard-word tree had falled into the river and sent all the water in to the Kapilavastu fields, leaving the Koli lands without any means of irrigation. The inhabitants of the two districts were unable to remedy this disaster, and a great feud had arisen. According to one account the Buddha, on his arrival, restored peace and harmony by good

---

[23] V. Smith, in Journal R.A.S.,loc. cit.

[24] Shih-erh-yu-ching (Bun., No. 1,374, tr. 392); Samyut. Nik., iii, p. 5; iv, p. 124.

advice. But according to another version of the story he hurled the tree of offence up in the air and caused it to divide, one half falling on the Kapilavastu side of the river and one on the Koli side. Rockhill gives Kalyanagarbha as the Sanskrit name of the tree, but we learn from the "Chung-hsu-ching" that it was Sara (or Sala)-kalyana. This name is translated by I-ching-shan-chien, good-solidity. We find mention also of a town Lohita, or Lohitaka, visited by Buddha, which was probably on this river. Some authors make the Rohita to be the boundary between the Kapilavastu territory and that of Sravasti. In one text of the 'Anagata-vamsa" we have the Banyan Arama placed on a river called the Rohani, but this is apparently a mistake.[25]

Another river in this country was the A-lu-na, or Aruna, which formed the boundary between the Magadha country and the territory of the Sakyas.[26]

At no great distance from Kapilavastu was a place in which one treatise is called the town of Ni-k'an, that is, perhaps, Nigama or Nirgama. In another work, however, it is called the Mi-chu-lu-yuan, that is, the Park (or Arama) of the hut of the strayed Lord. The Buddha is represented as lodging in a vihara here on one occasion near the close of his career.[27] We read also of the Sakya town Mi-lu-li, perhaps Mirul or Mirut, a place of some importance with a park and a monastery. Ha-li, or K'a-li, was another Sakyan town of some note. It had a vihara in which the great Sthavira

25 Chung-hsu-ching, ch. 4. The full title is Fo-shuo-chung-hsu-mo-ha-ti-ching (Bun., No. 859, tr. about 1000); Rockhill, op.cit., pp. 20, 52, Sarvata Vin. P'o-seng-shih, ch. 9; Fausholl's Dh., p. 351; Thera-gatha, v. 529 (P.T.S.); Journal P.T.S., 1886, p. 53.

26 Chung-pen-ch'i-ching, ch. 1 (Bun., No. 556, tr. 207).

27 Vibhasha-lun, ch. 13; Abhidharma-maha vibhasha-lun, ch. 105.

Katyayana resided, and Buddha once lodged here and was visited by King Prasenajit.[28] Other Sakya towns of which we find mention in the Buddhist scriptures are Ulumpa,[29] Chatuma, [30] Khomadussa,[31] and one called in Chinese 'Yellow Pillow.'[32] A town which in the Chinese texts is Shih-chu, Stone-Lord, that is, Silapati, is evidently that which in Pali is called Silavati.[33] We read also of the towns of Nava, in Chinese Na-ho (in one place Na-ssu by mistake),[34] Sakkara[35] (known only as a correct reading given in a note), and Karshaka or Ka-li-sha-ka.[36] This last word, which means ploughing, is the name of the town and district to which Suddhodana sent Siddhartha as chief magistrate. Here Siddhartha, sitting under a jambu-tree, watched the ploughers at their hard work, and gradually became absorbed in Samadhi. There was also the Sakya town called Ku-lo-p'i-ta-ssu, which perhaps stands for a name like Kaula-bhedas, meaning Family-dividing.[37] The Buddha once spent some time in this town, and during his visit had an interview with the presiding deity of the place. We find mention also of a town, apparently a busy trading centre, called Nyagrodhika, in Chinese 'the village of the tree with many roots.' This town was not far from Kapilavastu on the side

---

[28] Chung-a-han-ching, ch. 59; Tsa-a-han-ching, ch. 20; Fo-shuo-han-t'i-ching (Bun., No. 660, tr. about 290).

[29] Fausholl's Dh., p. 222.

[30] Maj. Nik., Vol. i, p. 456.

[31] Samyut, Nik., i, p. 184.

[32] Tsa-a-han-ching, ch. 27. The words are Huang-ch'en.

[33] Tsa-a-han-ching, ch. 39; Samyut. Nik., i, p. 116 ff.

[34] Ta-ai-tao-pi-chiu-ni-ching (Bun., No. 1,147, tr. about 400); Chung-pen-ch'i-ching, ch. 2.

[35] Samyut, Nik., i, p. 184.

[36] Chung-hsu-ching, ch. 4.

[37] Pie-i-tsa-a-han-ching, ch. 9 (Bun., No. 546, tr. about 400).

next Sravasti, and it had a large banyan capable of giving shelter to 500 waggons with room to spare. The Buddha once went to this place from Rajagriha and stayed in it for some time. In this town was a Brahmin, whose wife, a Kapilavastu woman, gave alms to Buddha, and received from him the prophecy that in a future birth she would become a Pratyeka-Buddha.[38]

Among the mountains of the Sakya country was one which was the home of the aged seer Asita. In the "Chung-hsu-ching" this mountain is called Kin-shih-ki-t'e,[39] and it is apparently the Kishkindha of Schiefner and the Sarvadhara of Rockhill. There was also the Chung-sheng or Bell-sound Mountain, with a village of the same name, the home of the family to which Buddha's wife Gopa belonged. This "Bell-sound" is apparently the Kinkinisvara of Rockhill and the Gantasabda (Ghantasabda), with a similar meaning, of Schiefner, the man's name being that of his home.[40]

Not very far from Kapilavastu was a wood with a river and village adjoining. This neighbourhood became celebrated as the place at which, according to some accounts, Prince Siddhartha made his first halt in his flight from home. The wood and the district are called in Chinese texts A-nu-ye, and A-nu-mi-ka-ya, and A-yu hamlet or A-nu wood. It is also called the A-nu-mo country, and is placed 480 li (about 95 miles) from Kapilavastu. The river is called in the Pali books Anoma or Anaya or Annana. In this neighbourhood was the district called Mi-ni-ya, the home of the brothers

---

38 Divyavadana, p. 67. The story is given from the same source in the "Sarvat Vinaya Yao-shih", ch. 8. This treatise, not being in the Ming Collection of Buddhist books, is not in Bunyio Nanjio's Catalogue.

39 Chung-hsu-ching, ch. 3; Rockhill, op. cit., p. 18, and note.

40 Sarvata Vin. P'o-seng-shih, ch. 3; Rockhill, op.cit., p. 21.

Mahanama and Aniruddha. The Buddha sojourned for a second time here when he came to pay his first visit to his native place as Buddha, and here he formally admitted Upali and the young Sakya gentlemen into his Order.[41]

Near Kapilavastu there was a park or wood called Lu-t'i-lo-ka, from the name of the presiding deity. This park was a favourite resort of the young Siddhartha, and there was in it a particular stone on which he was accustomed to sit. When Yasodhara is accused of having been unfaithful to her absent husband, she carries her little son Rahula to this wood and places him on the stone. Then, in the presence of Prajapati and other relatives, she causes the stone with the baby on it to be cast into the river. The stone floats, and so the innocence of the mother and the legitimacy of the child are openly established. This Lu-t'i-lo-ka may stand for Rudhiraka, from rudhira, which means red.[42]

It has been seen that the Banyan Arama at Kapilavastu had apparently been used as a place of resort for religious purposes by the Sakyas before their conversion to Buddhism. Another shrine in the Sakya country also connected with the older religions is that called the Yu-lo-t'i-na-t'a, that is, perhaps, the Uradina Chaitya. The Buddha lodged here once, and during his stay was visited by the presiding deva of the place. No explanation of the name is given, but it may possibly be the Sanskrit form for Udena, the name of

---

41 Wu-fen Vin., ch. 15; Ssu-ten Vin., ch. 4; Hsiu-shing-pen-ch'i-ching, ch. 2; Hsing-chi-ching, ch. 58; Hardy, Manual of Buddhism, p. 164 (2nd ed.); Bigandet's Legend of the Buddha, i, p. 64; Rockhill, op.cit., p. 26.

42 Hsing-chi-ching, ch. 51.

a celebrated old chaitya supposed to have been in the Vaisali country. [43]

The Cities of the Buddhas Krakucandha and Konakamuni

According to the narratives of the Chinese pilgrims, the cities associated with the two past Buddhas Krakucandha (or Kakucandha, or Krakuchanda) and Konakamuni (or Kanakamuni, or Konagamano, or Konakamana) were apparently in the Sakya territory, but we have not any explicit statement to that effect. It is entirely to these narratives that we are indebted for our knowledge of the situations of these two cities, but the pilgrims do not quite agree on the subject.[44] Fa-hsien places Krakuchanda's city, which he calls Na-p'i-ka, twelve yojanas (about 96 miles) south-east from Sravasti, and so to the south-west of Kapilavastu. Yuan-chuang states that he went south from Kapilavastu 50 li (ten miles) to the tope at the old city, which was the birthplace of his Buddha. Then Fa-hsien places Konakamuni's city less than a yojana to the north of Na-p'i-ka and west of Kapilavastu, while Yuan-chuang places it 30 li (about six miles) north-east from Krakuchanda's city, and so to the south-east of Kapilavastu.[45]

In a passage of I-ching's translation of the "Sarvata Vinaya" we find that the Buddha, when proceeding from Kapilavastu to Sravasti, goes to the town P'i-shu-na-lo and thence to Ku-na, or Kona, the city of the Buddha Konagamamuni.[46]

---

[43] Tsa-a-han-ching, ch. 22.

[44] Fo-kuo-chi, ch. 21; Hsi-yu-chi, loc. cit.

[45] Nabhika seems to have been known as the name of a place. In the "Hsing-chi-ching" (ch. 51) we have mentioned of a senior bhikshu who is called Senayana of Na-p'i-ka.

[46] Sarvata Vin. Yao-shi, ch. 7.

The "Fo-ming-ching" calls Krakuchanda's city Wu-wei or fearless, which may be a rendering of Na-p'i-ka, that is, Nabhika.[47] But the Chinese words may also stand for Abhaya with the same meaning. Other names for this Buddha's city, but always without indication of situation, are Lun-ho (or ha)- li-t'i-na,[48] An-ho,[49] and Ch'a-mo,[50] Kshama, or Kshema. The word kshama, which means 'earth,' means also 'endurance' or 'patience,' and Kshema means 'peace' or 'security,' and the latter word may have been the original for An-ho, which has a similar meaning.

The city of the Kanakamuni Buddha is also called Ch'a-mo-yue-ti or Kshamavati.[48] Other names for it are Shu-p'o-fu-ti[50] or Subhavati, Chuang-yen,[47] meaning Adorned or Well-furnished, and Ch'ing'ching,[49] meaning Pure. These two Chinese terms may have been given as renderings for Subhavati, which is used in the sense of beautiful and pure.

The ruins of two of the topes in honour of these two Past Buddhas have lately, as we know, been discovered in Nepal. The site of the city and the tope of Krakuchanda were found seven miles south-west from the supposed site of Kapilavastu. Kanakamuni's tope was found near the tank of the village of Nigliva. Near the latter tope is a stone pillar with an inscription which records that King Piyadassi (Asoka) increased the stupa of the "Buddha Konakamana for the second

---

47 Fo-shuo-Fo-ming-ching, ch. 8 (Bun., No. 404, tr. about 400). Cf. Mahawamsa, p. 57.

48 Ch'i-Fo-fu-mud-hsing-tzu-ching (Bun.,No. 626, tr. about 530).

49 Chang-a-han-ching, ch. 1.

50 Ch'i-Fo-ching (Bun., No. 860, tr. about 975). So the Sapta Buddha Stotra calls the birthplace of Krakuchanda Kshemavati and that of Kanakamuni Sobhanavati.

time."[51] If this pillar had been actually set up by Asoka I think he would have stated on it that he first erected and afterwards increased the tope to the Past Buddha. We do not seem to have any reason for believing that there was any tope to Kanakamuni before Asoka's time. It was probably not until the teachings of the Buddha had lost much of their spiritual and allegorical meaning that topes and cities were assigned to the Past Buddhas. These beings were the spiritual forefathers of the Buddha, and their "old cities" were their teachings of the Four Truths and the Eightfold Way.[52] The topes also to their memory were not made by mortals, and were not on this earth: they were in Fairyland, in Nowhere Country, and were made by devas. Thus Kanakamuni, who was eight miles (25 yojanas) in height, had a tope which covered eighty miles. It was in a blissful region, full of shady trees and fragrant flowers, with cool, clear tanks; the haunt of tuneful birds, and the home of heavenly maidens, who with dance and song made endless delight. On the walls of its numerous chambers were portrayed in clear, bright colours the manifold vicissitudes of the aeonian lives of the devas in heaven, and hell, and on earth; the truthful representations of inflexible unfailing Karma. And after the manner of this tope was that to Krakuchanda, and apparently neither was ever seen by a human mortal. The devas worshipped at them, and the King of the wild geese, Good-time by name, at Krakuchanda's tope chanted the merits of that Buddha in high-piping Pali understood by all who heard him.[53] It is interesting to note that the magnificent tope to the honour of Krakuchanda at the place of his

---

[51] Academy, April 27, 1985.

[52] Fo-shuo-chiu-chiu-ch'eng-yu-ching (Bun., No. 902, tr. about 990).

[53] Cheng-fa-nien-ch'u-ching, chs. 47-52 (Bun., No. 678, tr. 539); cf. also ch. 43.

cremation was feigned to have been made by a king called Asoka.[54]

The Destruction of Kapilavastu

The invasion of Kapilavastu and the destruction of the city and extermination of its inhabitants by King Virudhika form a curious and interesting narrative. The different versions of the story present some important differences of detail as to the circumstances which preceded and led to the invasion, but there is a tolerable agreement as to its principal incidents and its results. We find the narrative in the "Avadana Kalpalata," the Pali "Jataka" and the Commentary on the "Dharmapada," in the Tibetan Dulva treatise translated by Mr. Rockhill, and in several Chinese translations of canonical books. It is from one of these, the Sarvastivadin (or Sarvata) Vinaya, as translated by I-ching, that the following summary of the story has been condensed.[55]

There was a certain Sakya named Mahanama, a rich landlord possessing lands and villages. He had an agent or steward who was a Brahmin, and by a Brahmin wife was the father of a son and daughter. In course of time the agent died owing a large sum of money on account of rents and dues to his landlord, who took the daughter in satisfaction of his claim. This handsome, accomplished young girl accordingly became a slave in Mahanama's household, and her business was to attend to the flowers and make garlands. On this account her original name was dropped and she was called Malika, the Garland-maker. But her name is commonly given as Mallika (in Chinese Mo-li), which denotes a king of jasmine.

---

[54] Divyavadana, p. 418.

[55] Sarvata Vin. Tsa-shih, chs. 7, 8 (Bun., No. 1,121, tr. 710).

Now it came to pass that one day Prasenajit, King of Kosala, while out on a hunting expedition, became separated from his retinue and strayed into Mahanama's garden. Here he met Mallika, who showed such thoughtful kindness in getting him water and enabling him to have a safe and quiet sleep that the king fell in love with her. On learning her position he demanded her from her master, who replied that Mallika was only a slave-girl and that there were many Sakya maidens better than she. The King, however, wanted Mallika, and so she was sent to him and he made her his queen.

The marriage seems to have been a very happy one, and in due time Mallika bore Prasenajit a son, who, on account of bad omens which preceded his birth, was called Ill-born—in Sanskrit, Virudhika. At the time of this prince's birth a great statesman of Kosala had a son born to him, and this child was named K'u-mu or Mother-distressing—in Sanskrit, Dukhamatrika—the Ambarisha of Rockhill. These two boys grew up together at Sravasti as playmates and friends. It happened that on one occasion they were out on a hunting expedition and wandered into the Sakyas' Park, near Kapilavastu. When the young Sakyas heard of this they became very angry, abused Virudhika as the son of a slave-girl, and were with difficulty restrained from violence. The Prince escaped, and he made a vow to his companion that as soon as he became king he would return to the city and wreck vengeance on the inhabitants for the insult.

The years went by and Virudhika succeeded to the throne of Kosala, and immediately proceeded to prepare for taking revenge on the Sakyas of Kapilavastu. Having collected his troops and put himself at their head, he was on his way to attack that city when a

A unique type of Buddhist chaitya about 100 years old, Siddhapokhari

word from the Buddha softened him and turned him back. This was repeated, but at last the Buddha left his kinsmen to the working of their irremediable karma, and Virudhika, goaded on by his ruthless companion, carried out his invasion. After some fighting and much intriguing he became master of the city.

Hereupon he proceeded to carry out his long-delayed purpose of revenge for the wanton insult in the Park. His orders were that all the Sakya inhabitants, old and young, male and female, should be put to death. These commands were being carried out in a pitiless savage manner, and many thousands had been butchered, exception being made in favour of Mahanama and his family. Then Mahanama interceded for his countrymen, and obtained an order for a stay of the massacre for so long as he should be in the tank performing his ablutions preparatory to a conference. He then went into the water, tied his hair to the root of a tree, and drowned himself. The King was enraged when he discovered the trick, and ordered the carnage to be renewed. He demolished the city, massacred or drove away all its inhabitants, and then went back to his capital. But the punishment of his crime quickly overtook him, and a few days after his return he went in the fire of his fate down into hell.

This version of the story agrees in the essential points with the "Avadana Kalpalata" [56] and the Tibetan Vinaya,[57] but it differs in several particulars from the other versions. The Tibetans translate the name of the invader by "noble born" or "the high-born one." In Pali his name appears under the forms Vidudabha and Vitatubha, and a form Vidudha perhaps gave the

---

56 Journal Buddhist Society, vol. iv, pt. 1, p.5.

57 Rockhill, op.cit. p. 74 ff.

Chinese Liu-li as if for Vaidurya. According to the Pali accounts[58] and the "Tseng-i-a-han-ching,"[59] when King Prasenajit's messengers demand one of their daughters from the Sakyas of Kapilavastu to be his queen, Mahanama cleverly passes off his own daughter by a slave-girl as his legitimate daughter. The messengers are deceived and take the girl to the King, who receives her with great ceremony and makes her his queen. The "Wu-fen Vinaya,"[60] which also makes Prasenajit send to the Sakyas for one of their daughters, represents Mahanama as, with cunning guile, sending a slave-girl from his own household, and this was the version known to the Chinese pilgrim Yuan-chuang. These versions of the story of the marriage in which trickery is practised on the King are not only very absurd, but they are also inconsistent with the sequel of the narrative.

In the Pali stories, the "Wu-fen Vinaya," and some other treatises it was the violent conduct of the Sakya to Virudhika on account of his thoughtless use of their new Hall which made him vow revenge. The Sakyas had recently built a fine new Assembly Hall in or near their city, and they had agreed that it was not to be used by anyone whatever until it had been formerly opened by the Buddha.[61] In the meantime, before this opening occurred, Prince Virudhika, a boy, comes to Kapilavastu with his retinue and instals himself in the Hall. Hearing of this the Sakyas become very angry, and had not the Prince fled they would might have treated him with violence. As he had gone they contended themselves with abusing him as the

58 Fausboll's Dh., p. 211 ff.; Hardy''s Manual of Buddhism, p. 293; Jataka, vol. iv, p. 144; Fick's Soc. Gliederung im N. Indien Zu Buddha's Zeit' p. 30.

59 Tseng-a-han-ching, ch. 26.

60 Wu-fen Vin., ch. 21.

61 Liu-li-wang-ching; Wu-fen Vin., loc. cit.

Bajrajogini at Sankhu

son of a slave-girl, took up the tiles of the floor, and purified with milk and water the benches (or slabs) he had occupied. The personal force of the insulting term "son of a slave-girl" which the hot-tempered young Sakyas used to the Prince appears less when we recall that the same term was applied by the Sakyas to his father. Moreover this P'usa, while he was in Tushita Paradise, had declared that Virudhika's grandfather was of an impure family, being of Matanga blood. The Sakyas, however, were guilty of the offence of abusing—akrosamana—Prince Virudhika, calling him bad names.[62]

All versions of the story agree in representing King Virudhika as treating Mahanama during the invasion with great respect and kindess. He calls him by names like Grandfather or Maternal-grandfather, and the "Liu-li-wang-ching" makes the King to be much moved by Mahanama's patriotism in dying for his fellow-citizens.[63] According to that work the King, on learning the circumstances, stops the massacre, takes charge of the children, appoints a new governor, and goes away. But the Pali story makes Mahanama despise Virudhika, the alien, to the end, and drowned himself to escape the loathed hospitality of the King. In all accounts, however, Mahanama is the chief among the Sakyas of the Kapilavastu district. He is styled as King by the bhikshus and General by Virudhika, he is the father of Gopa; the friend of King Prasenajit and his son, and also of the Buddha. In the "Avadana Kalpalata" his name is not mentioned, and he is merely called "the great Sakya chief."

---

62 Abhidharma-maha vibhasha-lun, ch. 14; see also chs. 83, 105; Vibhasha-lun, ch. 13.

63 Ssu-fen Vin., ch. 41; Liu-li-wang-ching.

The story of the destruction of Kapilavastu and the massacre of its inhabitants by Virudhika is evidently of an old date. We find reference to the events of it in the "Vibhasha-lun" and the "Abhidharma-ta-vibhasha-lun," the former attributed to Sitavana or Katyayanaputra and the latter to the arhats of Kanishka's Council. These treatises quote the same passage from an earlier and now unknown sutra. According to this authority, Ananda went with another disciple to see Kapilavastu on the day after the departure of Virudhika. We read that Ananda was greatly affected by the ruin and desolation he found. The city was like a cemetery: the walls of the houses had been demolished and doors and windows destroyed; the gardens, and orchards, and lotus-ponds were all ruined; the birds made homeless were flying about in confusion; the only human beings to be seen were the orphaned children, who followed Ananda with piteous cries for help and compassion.[64] Deeply grieved, Ananda contemplated the fragments of the 70,000 (or 100,000). Sakya men who had been trodden to death by elephants and their bodies torn to pieces by harrows in the park near the Sow's Tank. In other treatises also we read that Virudhika practically annihilated Kapilavastu and exterminated the Sakyas of that city. Beginning with children at the breast, we are told, he slew all the Sakyas and washed the stone slabs of the Hall with their blood as he had vowed to do. The total number of the massacred is given as 99,900,000 in one treatise, and from this the absurd total has been quoted by others. Yet the monks seem to have remained uninjured, and some of the people were left unhurt, while a

---

[64] Vibhasha-lun, ch. 11, and references under note 2, p. 557.

portion fled into Nepal.[65]

It is hard to accept the story of the sacking of Kapilavastu and the extermination of its inhabitants by Virudhika, who, as king of Kosala, was also the King of Kapilavastu. Was the story made up in order to get rid of the impossible city invented by the makers of the romances about the Buddha's birth and early life? There are many and strong assumed to be true and known in several treatises, and some of the incidents are related as the occasions on which certain Vinaya rules were made. Thus, the giving of garments to needy brethren, the prohibition against the wearing of jewellery by bhikshunis, and the permission to ordain boys of seven years of age are all referred to the state of affairs at Kapilavastu immediately after its destruction by Virudhika.[66] When Ananda went to visit the bhikshus, who had fled from the massacre into a cold district of Nepal, he found them protecting themselves against the frost by the use of the fu-lo which the natives wore. He considered himself bound by rules not to wear this, and so he returned to Sravasti with skin rough and chappy. Hearing of the circumstances, the Buddha made a new rule allowing the use of fu-lo in cold countries. The meaning of fu-lo is not given, but it is probably the Sanskrit vala, which means the hair or coarse wool of animals used for clothing. [67] Then in the very interesting Dhammapada treatise called "Ch'h-yao-ching," translated in 399, we find

---

[65] Ta-pan-nie-p'an-ching, chs. 14, 36 (Bun., No. 114, tr. about 430); I-tsu-ching, ch. 2; Mahasanghika Vin., ch. 30 (Bun., No. 1,119, tr. 416); Sarvasti-vada Vinaya-vibhasha, ch. 7 (Bun., Nos. 1,135, 1,136, tr. 400).

[66] Shi-sung Vinaya, ch. 21 (Bun., No. 1,115, tr. 404); Wu-fen Vin., ch. 21.

[67] Sarvata Vin. P'i-ko-shih, ch. 2 (translated by I-ching about 715, not in Bunyio). I-ching mentions an old rule that "fu-lo does not enter the Hall of Fragrance," that is, Buddha's temple (Nan-hai-ch'i-kuei, etc.,

Virudhika's punishment of the Sakyas introduced in order to enforce and illustrate the doctrine of Karma. The verse to which the reference forms a comment declares that "not in the air nor in the ocean nor entering the mountain-cave—it is impossible in these places to escape the punishment of bad Karma."[68] Again, in the "Sarvata-vini-vibhasha," translated into Chinese about A.D. 400, we find a reference to the mutilation and massacre of the Sakyas by Virudhika. The writer introduces the reference in illustration of Buddha's power in mercy and kindness as he healed and comforted the wretched victims.[69]

When the Buddha went to see the ruin and desolation caused by Virudhika's army he professed to be and apparently was unmoved, being freed from earthly grief, but he confessed that the sight gave him a headache. The headache he connected with unbecoming conduct in one of his former existences. In this particular existence, while he was a small boy, he came one day to a place where a body of fishermen had taken the fish from a pond and cruelly left them to die on the banks. The little boy rapped one of the fish wantonly on the head with a stick. As this fish lay dying beside a brother fish the two vowed to come back into the world at the same time and have revenge. The cruel fishermen became the Sakyas of Kapilavastu, the two fishes were reborn as Virudhika and his

---

[68] Ch'u-yao-ching, ch. 11 (Bun., No. 1,321, tr. 399), and cf. Fausboll's Dh., v, 127. There are further references to Virudhika's invasion in ch. 25 and other parts of the "Ch'u-yao-ching," which is an interesting Dhammapada treatise.

[69] Sarvastivada Vin. Vibhasha, loc. cit. In the Sarvata Vin. Tsa-shih, ch. 7, there is a pretty story of Mallika, the slave-girl, giving here own breakfast to Buddha. The compiler of the Pali "Questions of Milinda" spoils this story by making Mallika give, as alms to Buddha, some "last night's sour gruel." See Rhys Davids' "Questions of Milinda," iv, 8, 25.

friend, and although these could not kill Buddha, the little boy, they were able to cause him a bad headache.[70] Nor was the Buddha altogether master of his feelings as he seemed, for when he went to the Banyan Arama with the broken-hearted Ananda he sighed over the lonely desolation of the place. Then he went away declaring he would never return, and from that time Kapilavastu almost passed out of existence.

It is to be noted that the Pali and Mabasanghika Vinayas do not seem to have any mention of or reference to Virudhika's invasion and destruction of Kapilavastu. The latter treatise even tells of a congregation of Bhikshus at the city several years after Buddha's decease, and of a feud between Ananda and Rahula on account of an affair connected with a layman's children.[71] This estrangement had caused the regular services of the Church to cease for seven years, and a reconciliation was at last affected by the intervention of the aged Upali. But, on the other hand, to the Tibetan, the Ssu-fen, the Wu-fen, the Shih-sung, and Sarvata Vinayas the whole story of the invasion seems to be an accepted fact. Mr. Rhys Davids, following Bigandet, ascribes the destruction of Kapilavastu to Ajatasatru, the parricide king of Magadha. There is, however, evidently a mistake here, as there does not seem to be any authority for the statement.[72]

Conclusion

As we read the various Buddhist books composed at different times and at places wide apart, we seem to find in them three Kapilavastus or birth-places of the Sakya Buddha.

---

[70] Hsing-ch'i-hsing-ching, ch. i (Bun., No. 733, tr. about 195); Journal Bud. Soc., op.cit., p. 11.

[71] Mahasanghika Vin., ch. 30.

[72] Bigandet, op.cit., p. 267; R.Davids' Buddhism, p. 77.

We have first the Kapilavastu of the legends and romances, and the narratives based on these. This city, as has been seen, was supposed to be in the Happy Land of the Himavan, or region of the Snow Mountains, either on their south side or away north to the east of the Gandhamardana Mountain.[73] The site of this city was a pleasant one, full of natural charms, and impregnated with secret influences conducive to happiness and prosperity. The city was adorned with parks and gardens and ponds and palaces, and it was a heaven on earth.[74] At some distance from it was the Lumbini Garden, not a mere "Sal Park" or ordinary garden, with beautiful trees and lovely sweet-scented flowers, and tanks of clear cool water. It was a place even more than divine, for here gods worked at the behests of a higher but unknown power. Everything in it, animate and inanimate, knew when the fulness of the time for the Buddha's appearance had come. At the moment when the great event occurred, the flowers in the garden bloomed out of season the trees were covered with ornaments not their own, the very soil owned the presence of the great power, and unseen gods filled the air and tended the babe born to be a saviour.

It is probable that all Buddhists believed in the actual existence of this Kapilavastu with its Lumbini Garden. It is useless, however, to conjecture where the writers of the romances wished their readers to suppose the city to be situated. From the first it was little known to the Church, and even to the early writers Kapilavastu seems to be vague, uncertain place. In the "Digha Nikaya" and the "Sumangala Vilasini" we have a

---

73 Hsiu-hsing-pen-ch'i-ching, ch. 2.

74 Fang-kuang-ta-chuang-yen-ching, ch. 2 (Bun., No. 159, tr. 683); Abhidharma-maha vibhasha-lun, ch. 83.

record of a conversation which occurred in Kosala between the Buddha and a Brahman named Ambattha. In this the Buddha speaks of the city which was supposed to be his native place as if it were far away and a matter of old story.[75] The Lumbini Garden is not properly the place of Buddha's birth, but of his first appearance in the last stage of his existence. As the scene of his entrance on his last life, it is apparently of later invention than Kapilavastu. At least, it is not known to all the authors, and in the "I-ch'u-P'u-sa-pen-ch'i-ching," for example, there is no mention of it in the narrative of the Buddha's birth. It is also remarkable that when Asoka was taken by Upagupta to the Lumbini Garden, there was apparently no monument or memorial to mark the place. Asoka set up a tope at the place pointed out to him, and this was the first structure erected to indicate the Lumbini Garden.

We have next the Kapilavastu and Lumbini Garden, visited first by Asoka and afterwards by the Chinese pilgrims, and now rediscovered. This Kapilavastu, which seems to suit some of the narratives in the Buddhist scriptures, may also be the place with that name from which the Indian monk Dharmapala in the second century A.D. brought to China two Sanskrit MSS. These were translated into Chinese with the titles "Ching-pen-ch'i-ching" and "Hsiu-hsing-pen-ch'i-ching."[76] They are short treatises giving an account of a part of the Buddha's life, and they have been used by the present writer. But we have no records of any other pilgrims visiting this place, or of any great Buddhists residing as it, or of any human

---

75 Digha Nik., i, p. 92; Sumang. Vil., p. 258 (T.T.S.). The same story is to be found in the Sarvata Vin. Yao-shi, ch. 8.

76 Kao-seng-chuan, ch. 1.

life, except that mentioned by the two pilgrims, at it between the Buddha's time and the present. No doubt pilgrims went to the place and worshipped and wrote their names on topes or columns, but they did not tell of their pilgrimages to the sacred sites, nor did others write their stories for them. So far as we know, this Kapilavastu has never been seen by anyone as a city or even as a heap of ruins. A few lay inhabitants and a small congregation of Buddhist monks were the only residents in the district when it was visited by the Chinese pilgrims. The foundations of what was supposed to have been the old city wall were pointed out to Yuan-chuang, and he saw a well and a temple. If this last had survived, as the pilgrim in his simple faith believed, from the Buddha's birth-time its god had been changed, the Yaksha who gave increase to the Sakyas having been replaced by Siva. But, with a very few exceptions like these, topes and chaityas built long after the Buddha's death and monkish traditions have since the first visit been the only evidence for the identification of sites and objects with certain descriptions in the Buddhist books. The Asoka pillars and the remains of old topes found by the Nepalese in the Paderia district of the Terai are doubtless as seen by the two Chinese pilgrims, but we are not obliged to believe that they are at the places where the historical Buddha was born and spent his youth. Buhler, however, and Oldenberg, with other learned students of Buddhism, seem to be thoroughly convinced that these monuments indicate the sites of the objects mentioned in the Buddhist scriptures as connected with the birth and early years of the Buddha.[77] This conviction may be regarded as based on the supposition that Asoka and the Chinese pilgrims saw a large

[77] Buhler, op.cit.,p. 5; Oldenberg, op.cit., p. 110 ff; Waddell, in Journal As. Bengal, vol. lxv, pt. 1. No. 3, p. 275.

quantity of ruins at the place which they were told represented Buddha's Kapilavastu. But this supposition is not warranted by the Asoka legend or the narratives of the pilgrims. In these we have sites and chaityas with images or pictorial representations, but very few ruins of ancient buildings.

The third Kapilavastu is the actual place at which the Buddha was born and educated as a boy. We must remember, however, that the honour of having been the Buddha's birthplace has been claimed also for other cities, such as Sravasti and Kusinagara, and that the former of these was evidently a sort of home for him and some of his kindred. [78] Practically, however, there is a general agreement that his native place was called Kapilavastu or Kapilanagara. As we have seen, the books vary as to its situation with reference to other localities, and it does not seem to be possible at present to form a satisfactory and definite opinion as to its precise situation. There are, however, various reasons for regarding it as having been probably in the territory of the Vrijjians and not far from Rajagriha of Magadha. It was probably a small unimportant town, and its original name may have been something like Saka. We have already seen that Kapilavastu is placed by some writers in the Vrijjian territory and not far from Pava, an important town of those people.[79] We eal also of the Buddha going with his 1,250 disciples from Kapilavastu through the Vrijjian region to Vaishali.[80] The relations between the people of this district and the Buddha and his kinsmen seem to have been very intimate. According to some accounts the elephant which Devadatta in his sulky displeasure

[78] Chang-a-han-ching, ch. 3; Fan-i-ming-i, ch. 3.

[79] See also Ta-an-p'an-shuo-i-ching, ch. 1 (Bun., No. 681,tr. about 150)

[80] Chung-pen-ch'i-ching, ch. 2.

killed at a gate of the city of Kapilavastu, had been sent by the Vaisalians as a present to Prince Siddhartha. Moreover, some of the Buddha's relatives seem to have lived in or near Vaishali all their lives, or at least from the time they entered in Order. Ananda also is represented as having had an intimate friend among the Mallas of Pava while he was a young layman. After the Buddha's decease, moreover, Ananda went to live at Vaishali, and it was from that city that he and the arhats, according to one account, went to Rajagriha to attend the first Council.[81] Then we read of Mallas[82] and Lichchavis among the population of the Sakya district, and also of Lichchavi Sakyas. We may note, in passing, that when Yuan-chuang was at Vaishali he was informed that the hereditary King of Nepal was a Lichchavi Buddhist.

As to Rajagriha, it is very evident from some of the Buddhist books that their authors regarded it as not very distant from Kapilavastu. When the prince Siddhartha went out into the world, his first halt, according to several accounts, was, as has been observed, at Anuya (or Anomya), which was near to Rajagriha, and, according to some, on leaving his home he went gradually south from the borders of Magadha to Rajagriha.[83] The Sakya town called Koli and Devadaha and by other names was, we have seen, not very far from Kapilavastu. This important town, it will be observed, is not mentioned by the Chinese pilgrims, but their silence may perhaps be explained. I think it is the place which they call Rama, and which is about forty miles to the east of the Lumbini Garden. At this place there was a celebrated tope over relics of the

[81] Ssu-fen Vin., chs. 41, 54.

[82] P'u-yao-ching, ch. 3.

[83] Wu-fen Vin., ch. 15; Ssu-fen Vin., ch. 31.

Buddha, and near it were certain memorials connected with his flight from home. Now in a certain Nirvana treatise we read of the Buddha going from Rajagriha to Pataliputra, and from that city east to the Koli (Kou-li, city, and thence on the Vaisali. In this passage we find as a synonym for Koli the name Hsi-yu, that is, joy, delight, in Sanskrit, Rama. In the "Maha-Parinibbana Sutta" we find the form Kotigama instead of Koli. This Sutta also tells us how "Ramagamika Koliya," the Koliyas of Ramagama, obtained a share of the Buddha's relics. They claimed this on the ground that they were Kshatriyas and that the Buddha had been of the same caste.[84] It was also to this Ramagama or Lo-ma-ts'un that the prince went direct from Kapilavastu, according to the "Hsing-chi-ching," when he had passed through the Pi-ye-lo gate of the city.[85] Then, according to Yuan-chuang's travels, Ramagrama lay between the Lumbini Garden and Kusinagara; and in the "Sarvata Vinaya," Buddha, going in the opposite direction, journeys from Kusinagara to Devadaha (Koli) and thence to the Lumbini Garden.[86] Further, Mr. Rockhill's Tibetan authority represents the prince, while still a resident at home, as going "into the cemetery of Rajagriha."[87] This may be a slip of the pen, but the place at which Siddhartha watched the ploughers as he sat under a tree was apparently not far from this city. We read also of Suddhodana being one of the Buddha's audience at Rajagriha, and it was near this city apparently that Suddhodana was cremated.[88] The

[84] P'an-ni-huan-ching, ch. 1 (Bun., No. 119, tr. between 317 and 420); Journal R.A.S., Vol. VII, p. 65, and Vol. VIII, p.259.

[85] Hsing-chi-ching, ch. 17.

[86] Sarvata Vinaya, Yao-shih, ch. 7.

[87] Rockhill, op.cit., p. 23.

[88] P'u-sa-sheng-man-lun, ch. 4 (Bun., No. 1,312, tr. between 960 and 1127). This "Jataka-mala" is a late work and of doubtful value.

city was one of the favourite resorts of the Buddha, and his preference for it was noted and explained by early Indian Buddhist writers.[89] Some of his disciples also sojourned here, and Upananda apparently settled permanently on the Griddhakuta Mountain.[90] Several texts put Kapilavastu a little or a considerable distance to the north of Rajagriha, but even when it is said to be on the side of the Snow Mountains, it is on the banks of the Ganges and not far from Magadha.[91]

To the Buddhist writers generally the Himavan or Snow Mountains, the fabled home of great rishis and of rare medicinal herbs, were of uncertain and varying location. Thus, in some texts we find them placed twelve yojanas from Kapilavastu in a north direction apparently,[92] in other texts they are to the east, and in a few they are to the south of that city. They were also regarded by some as near to Rajagriha, for the First Council, which was held at that city, is also described as having been held at the Snow Mountains.[93] So when we read in certain books of the Ganges being near Kapilavastu and the Snow Mountains, we are not obliged to regard it as far away among the Himalayas. It is, however, quite correct according to some Buddhist geography to place the Ganges in a very remote region to the north. It rises, we are told, in the Anavatapta Lake, and flows from that in an eastern direction. From the same lake the Indus flows south, the Oxus to the west, and the Sita to the north. When we read, however, of Kapilavastu being near the Bhagirathi or Ganges, we are to understand by these names the

---

89 Ta-chih-tu-lun, ch. 3

90 Ssu-fen Vin., ch. 14.

91 Sarvata Vin. Yao-shih, ch. 8; Divyadana, p. 548.

92 Chung-hsu-ching, ch. 5.

93 P'i-ni-mu-ching, ch. i (Bun., No. 1,138, tr. about 400).

actual well-known river so called in India proper. According to the "Hsing-chi-ching," the old seer Asita went to Kapilavastu from "Ganges-town" of Magadha in the "Che-p'an-ti" district of South India. In the "Mahavastu" also this rishi is represented as living not on the Snow Mountains but on the Vindhya range.[94] Then in this connection we are reminded of the story of Prince Suddhodana obtaining permission to have a second wife. He had been successful in repelling the invasion of Sakyan territory by bands of plunderers from the border mountains. These invaders were called Pandavas, and one of the large mountains in the vicinity of Rajagriha was called Pandava.[95] Moreover, we find it stated that the Buddha's birthplace was in the "Middle Country," the Madhya-desa, and we are also informed that Magadha is the country in which the Buddha was born.[96]

That there was a name like Saka or Sakya for Buddha's birthplace, appears probable from the use of these words in several Buddhist texts. According to the romances and legends, the banished princes who formed the Kapilavastu colony acquired the name Sakyas, or the clever ones, from their father's exclamation of surprised delight. This name, however, seems to have become the designation of a large tribe or people occupying a considerable extent of territory. But the place at which the first settlers took up their abode and built their town was at a Saka-sando or Teak Wood, and from this the town and inhabitants seem to have acquired the names Saka and Sakya. This supposition helps to explain the distinction which is

---

[94] Hsing-chi-ching, ch. 7; Mahavastu (ed. Senart), ii, p. 30.

[95] Rockhill, op.cit., p. 15; Hsing-chi-ching, ch. 22.

[96] Ta-chih-tu-lun, ch. 25.

Sukhabati Likeshwara
Seto Matsyendranath?

(Painting by Siddhimum Shakya)

plainly drawn in several books between Saka and Sakya. The former is the general term, embracing the latter and much more. Thus we read of Buddha staying among the Sakyas at Kapilavastu in the Banyan Arama, but we also find that he "travels about among the Sakyas to the Kapilavastu country," that he lodges in the "Sakya town Silapati" and "in Devadaha in the Sakya country." Both in the Pali and the Chinese versions of some treatises we find the "Sakiyani" or Sakyas of Kapilavastu distinguished from the "Kolyani" or Sakyas of Koli.[97] The Sakiya and Koliya also are often mentioned together, and the word Sakya is frequently employed in ways which show that its application is restricted to Kapilavastu. Thus it was the wanton insolence of the Sakyas of this city which led to Virudhika's invasion, and the operations of the invader were, according to all accounts, confined to the Sakyas of the city and suburbs. So in the story the "Sakiyanam dosa" or "pubbakamma" is the guilt or previous karma of the Sakyas of Kapilavastu and not of the Sakyas generally.[98] And when it is recorded that "Sakiyavamso Vidudabhena ucchinna," this means that the Kapilavastu Sakyas were exterminated by the King. The first word, we know, cannot mean, as Childers translates, the "Sakya royal line," nor the Sakya race.[99]

In one sutra we find this expression—"the Amalika Medicine-tree orchard of the Sakyas' she-i" or Sakya.[100] This passage, however, is evidently corrupt, and there

---

97 Thera-gatha, p. 56 (P.T.S.); Samyut, Nik., iii, pp. 5,91; Mahasanghika Vin., ch. 39, where we read of Sakya, Koli, Malla, and Licchavi bhikshunis all under Maha Prajapati.

98 Jataka, iv, p. 152; Fausboll's Dh., p. 223.

99 Fausboll's Dh., p. 225; Childers' Pali Dictionary, s.v

100 She-li-fu Mo-ha-Mu-lien-yu-ssu-chu-ching (Bun., No. 625, tr. about 195). In the later translation in ch. 41 of the Tseng-i-a-han-ching'' the word She-i does not occur.

is nothing in the text to prove that She-i here means Kapilavastu. But Buddha uses the term Sakya to designate his native place, and we find it expressly stated that the name (Shi-ka) is a synonym for Kapilavastu.[101] Then we read of the She-i-lu or She-i-road, which the context shows is the road to Kapilavastu,[102] and Suddhodana is called "King of She-i."[103]

The word Sakya came to mean also a relative of Buddha, a member of the Kapilavastu family to which the Buddha was supposed to being, and so we sometimes find it interchanged with Gautama.[104] It also came to be used in the sense of "a Buddhist," and even in early times we find a woman declaring her separation from the Buddhist Church in the words "fei-Shi-chung-tsu," that is, "I am no more of the Sakya stock. "[105]

The derivations and explanations given in the books for Sakya do not seem to be very satisfactory. it is interesting to observe, however, that the inhabitants of Kapilavastu are connected with the Saka or Teak tree, and those of Devadaha with the Koli or Jujube tree. But Saka was possibly the name of the real or fictitious founder of the family of the Sakyas. To some writers these are the clan otherwise called by the name Gautama, and to some they were evidently the Kshatriyas. In relating the origin and history of the

---

[101] Fen-pie-kung-te-lun, ch. 2 (Bun., No. 1,290, trs. about 150, or according to others about 380); Ssu-fen Vin., chs. 3, 31.

[102] Chung-pen-ch'i-ching, ch. 1.

[103] Ching-fan-wang-pan-nie-p'an-ching, ch. 1 (Bun, No. 732, tr. 455).

[104] Vinaya (ed. Oldenberg) Mah., i, 38, ll; Tsa-a-han-ching, ch. 41; Samyut, Nik., iv, p. 183.

[105] Mahasanghika Vin., chs. 19, 37.

Kshatriya caste, Buddha and his followers merely talk about the mythical origin and descent of the Buddha's family. It may be worthy of investigation, however, whether Saka is not originally a foreign word meaning the marshy land or uet country, and Sakya the inhabitant of the country. This word may have been one of that large number of terms common to several old languages of Central Asia and still preserved to us in Chinese. One of the renderings given for the name of Buddha's native place is, as has been seen, Red Marsh. Now the word for marsh in Chinese is Tse, very like Shi or Sak, and formerly pronounced Teh and Sak. The word for uet or moist in Chinese in also Shi, and it also formerly had a pronunciation like sek or sak. The word Sak may have passed into the language of Indian and become confused with native words of similar sound. We have three Chinese versions made independently of a long and interesting sutra, the name of which was apparently the Maharudham sutra. In this work we have an account of the origin and descent of Buddha's family as Kshatriyas, and it is worthy of notice that there is no mention either of the banished princes or of Sakyas.[105]

105 Ta-lu-t'an-ching, ch. 6 (Bun., No. 551, tr. about 300). Mr. Bunyio gives the title as "Fo-shuo-lu-t'an-ching,"and suggests as its meaning "Sutra on the Lokadhatu spoken by Buddha." But "Ta-lu-t'an" is evidently for "Maharudham," meaning the great production, that is the origin of the world. In Nos. 549 and 550 the Sanskrit title is translated by "Ch'i-shih-yin-pen" and "Ch'i-shih" respectively.

Works on Nepal Buddhism

Adhikary, Suryamani — *"Kakrevihar Dekhi Rarasamma"* (From Kakre Vihar to Rura), *Madhuparka*, Vol. 12, No. 4. Aug. - Sept. 1979, pp. 95-105.

Adhikary, Suryamam, — *The Khasa Kingdom: A Trans-Himalayan Empire of Middle Age,* Nirala Publications. Jaipur, New Delhi

Badri Ratna, Ratnakazi Vajracharya — *Nepal Janajivan Kriya Paddhati*, Kathmandu, 1963, p. 38.

Deva, K. — *Buddhist Art and Architecture in India and Nepal*, Gangtok, Namgyal Institue of Tibetology, Vol. XI.

Hai Lai, Mr. — *"Arniko's Architectural Legacy", China Daily* quoted in Rising Nepal, November, 27, 1981.

Haimendorf, C. Von Furer (London) — *"A Nunnery in Nepal", Kailash,* Vol. IV. No. 2, 1976, pp. 121-154.

Hridaya, Chittadhar — *Dharmaditya Dharmacharya wa Napalbhasha wa Thwaya*

	Sahitrya, On Dharmaditya Dharmacharya and Newari language and literature, in Newari Nepalbhasha Sahitya Gosthi, Calcutta, 1964, p. 46.
Keith Dowman	*The Legend of the Great Stupa of Boudhanath,* Translated from the Tibetan Terma of Sngags Chang Sakya Bzang Po, Illustrated by Glen Eddy, A Diamond Sow Publication, 2nd edition, Kathmandu, 1978. p. 52.
Lakaul, Vaikuntha Prasad (ed.)	*Buddha Dharma wa Nepal Bhasha Muna,* On Nepal Buddhism and Newari literature, Kathmandu, 1972.
Lama, Colonel Santabir	*Nangba Sange,* On different aspects of Lamaistic Buddhism in Nepali, vs. 2021, Kathmandu, p. 111.
Mary Slusser	*Nepala Mandala,* A cultural study of the Kathmandu Valley, Vol. 1, text Princeton University Press, New Jersy 1982, p. 491. Vol. 2, Plates, 599 Plates.
Pal, Dr. Pratapaditya	*Two Buddhist Paintings from Nepal,* Museum Van Aziatische Kunst/Rijks Museum, Amsterdam, Legacy of Mr. P. Spies, 1967, p. 43.
Panta, Dinesh Raj	*Additional Remarks on the*

Traditions of the date of Lord Buddha, English and Nepali, Lumbini Development Committee, HMG Kathmandu, Lumbini year 1979, p. 13.

Panta, Mahesh Raj — *"Pushyabhishek"*, (a type of coronation), having references to the Medieval period, Purnima, Samshodhan Mandal, No. 33, VS 2032 Bhadra, pp. 13-27.

Paudel, Nayanath — *"Langtang Gaunko Raja Jaya Prakasha Mallako Tamrapatra"*, Sandarbha, No. 1. 2035. Ed. Mohan Prasad Khanal, Parthamani Upadhayaya, pp. 71-72.

Man Pradhan, Jhulendra — *Nepal Bhasha Bakhan Sahitya ya Itihasa,* Chyasapasa, 1970: contains the following Buddhist stories in Newari:

i). Ashta Vaitaraga (pp. 55-62).

ii). Havari Kshambu - Lamarima Kshambu (pp. 81-82).

iii). Buddhaya Swinigu Janma (pp. 86-117).

Prajnananda Bhikshu — *Trilakkhanadipani,* Buddhist Sanskrit text translated into Newari, Sahu Bhajuratna, Kathmandu, 1951, p. 42.

Ram, Dr. Rajendra — *A History of Buddhism in Nepal (A.D. 704-1396)*, Janabharati Prakashan, Patna, 1977, p. 249.

Shakya, Hemaraj — *Shri Vidyadhari Vijayeshvaristhana*, Vijayeshvari Mahavihar Sudhar Samiti, 1979, p. 33.

Shakya, Hemaraj — *Nepal Samskritiya Mulukha*, On aspects of Nepalese and Buddhist cultures, Shrimati Laksmi Devi Shakya, Lalitpur Jayashri Vihar, 1969, p. 124, Newari.

Shakya, Hemaraj — *Buddhamurti Cchagu Adhyayan*, A Study on Buddhist images, Chwasapasa, Kathmandu, 1977. p. 101 + Appendices, Illustrated Newari.

Shakya, Hemaraj — *"Bauddha Grantha Swayambhu Puranantargata Ashta Vaitaraga Katha"*, The legend of Kumbheshvara as one of the Ashta Vaitaragas as contained in the Buddhist Swayambhu Purana, Kumbheshvara Itihasa, Sahu Bekhanath Shrestha Lalitpur Kobahal, VS 2018. pp. 1-4.

Shakya, Hemaraj — *Nepal Bauddha Vihar wa Granthasuchi* (List of Viharas and works of Nepalese Buddhism), Dharmodaya

	Sabha, Fourth World Buddhist Conference, Buddha Era 2500, p. 38.
Shakya, Hemaraj	*Shri Hiranyavarna Mahaviharsthita Pindapatra Abhilekh,* Malla Inscriptions on begging bowls from the Hiranyavarna Mahavihar Patan, Mukta Bahadur Dhakhwa, Pulchok, Patan, 1980. p. 36.
Shakya, Hemaraj	*Shri Bhaskarakirti Mahavihar* 'Yetakha Baha Cchagu Adhyayana', A study on Yetkha Vihar, Yetakha Baha Arya Namasangiti Guthi, Financed by Stationary Centre Juddha Sadak, 1979.p. 54.
Shakya, Hemaraj	*Shivadevasamskarita Shri Rudravarna Mahaviharasthita tala-patra abhilekha,* (Palm leaf inscriptions in the Rudravarna Mahavihar Patan), Buddhajayanti Samiti Ukubaha Patan, N.S. 1100 (1980),p. 28.
Shakya, Ratna Jyoti (Trans.)	*2524th Auspicious Birthday Ceremony of Lord Buddha,* 'The commemorable day for "The Light of Asia", The Enlightened one, *A Brief Introduction of Shivadeva Sanskarita Omkuli Shri Rudrav-*

	arna Mahavihar, Sangha Ratna Shakya, Hera Kazi Shakya, Bhima Ratna Shakya, organised: 2524th Rudravarna Mahavihar Improvement Committee Okhubahal Mahabauddha Lalitpur, Nepal, 1980. p. 26.
Sudarshan Bhikshu	*Padmapani Bodhisattwa*, Ratnaman Shakya Ashokman Shakya Nepal Craft Emporiu, Pulchok, Patan, 1979. p. 128.
Sudarshana Bhikshu (Edit.)	*Buddha, Buddha Dharma Sambandhi Grantha Suchi*, All Upasikas of Gana Mahavihar, Kathmandu, p. 23.
Upasak, Samyakratna	*Khwapade Bahabahiya Sankshiptta Parichaya*, (A brief introduction to Viharas of Bhaktapur) Dharmapasapin (followers of religion), Bhaktapur, 1971, p. 26.
Vajracharya, Adi	*Aitihasikaya Cchun Varnana*, (Some historical glimpses) Newari, (Kathmandu), 1958, p. 24.
Vajracharya, Amogha Vajra (Samshodhaka)	*Dharmashri Mitraya Sankshiptta Itihasa*, (A short history of Dharmashri Mitra), N.S. 1092, Shripanchami.
Vajracharya, Amogha Vajra	*Ashtottarashata Lokeshvara Parichaya* (Introduction to 108

	Lokeshvaras) 'Nepahdeya Kanakachaitya Mahaviharaya Ashttottarasata' (108 Lokeshvaras of Kanaka Chaitya Mahavihar (i.e. Macchendra Bahal) of Nepal country), Lokeshvara Sangh, N.S.1099 Madan Printing Press, Balkumari Ducchen, Yen (Kathmandu), p. 196 + 37.
Vajracharya, Ashakazi	*Bungadyo Nepale Hahgukhan Nepalbhashaya Vamshavali*, 'The History of Shree Karunamaya in Nepalbhasha', The story of Lord Matsyendranathas coming to Nepal, Jagat Uddhar Press, Kathmandu, 1965, p. 81.
Vajracharya, Ashakazi (Ganeshraj)	*Gunavati Katha*, 'The story of Gunabati in Nepal Bhasha', Patan 1972. p. 98.
Vajracharya, Ashakazi (Ganeshraj	*Sanhuguthiya Mahima Suradatta Katha*, The importance of the committee for funeral as illustrated by Suradatta's story known from genealogies, Patan, 1972. p. 93.
Vajracharya, Ashakazi	*Mahayana Buddha Dharma*, A section of Swayambhu Purana, A work on Tirthas of Nepal, Patan, 1971, p. 19.

Vajracharya, devananda *Swayambhu Darshan,* Poetic description of Swayambhu, Shubharatna Tamrakar, Kathmandu, 1963. p. 14: Newari.

Vajracharya, Devaratna *Dashavalastavam,* (Stutamapi) Sanskrit and Newari hyninical verses, Bhosikotol, Kathmandu undated.

Vajracharya, Jnanaratna *Shri Prajnaparamita Deviyagu Ekavimshati Shlokaya Bhashasahitam,* Twenty one verses of Prajna Paramita in Newari translation, Taramula Mahavihar, Kathmandu, 1919. p. 24.

Vajracharya Mana Bajra (Trans.) *Mythological History of the Nepal Valley from Swayambhu Purana,* Edited by: Smith, And *Naga and Serpent Symbolism by Warren W. Smith* Avolok Publishers Kathmandu, 1978. p. 78.

Vajracharya, Mohan Raj *Gokarneshvar Vitaragakatha,* NS 1100 (1980), Sanukazi Vajracharya, Bhinccha Vahah, Lalitpur, p. 21.

Vajracharya, Mohan Raj *Ashtami Vrata Katha,* On Astami Vrata ritual and story, from Uposhadhavadana, Hemaratna Vajracharya, Patan, 1975, p. 28 (Newari).

Vajracharya, Ratna Bahadur	*Gurumandalarchana wa Ekavimshati Prajna-Paramita,* On Tantric ritual based on Prajnaparamita text, with Newari translation, Gunaratna Shakya, Patron - Purna Bahadur Vajracharya, Patan, 1975, p. 34.
Vajracharya, Pt Ratna Bahadur	*Bauddha Prathama shiksha,* Written and translated, Patron: Purna Bahadur Vajracharya, Pub: Gunaratna Shakya, Lalitpur, 1972. p. 132.
Vajracharya, Ratnakazi (of Mantrasiddhi Mahivihar (Saval Bahal)	*Yen Deya Bauddha Puja Kriya ya Halanjvalan,* 'Materials required for the rituals of the Buddhists of Kathmandu, Nepal Buddha prakashan Kathmandu, 1980. p. 137.
Vajracharya, Vishvavajra	*Nepal Bhasha Deva Stotra,* Sanskrit and Newari hymns of Buddhist gods and goddesses, Ananda Bahal Patan, 1974. p. 44.
Vajracharya, Samyak Ratna	*Mallakalin Bauddha Kalakriti,* Bauddha Darshan Adhyayan Parishad, Bhaktapur 1979. p. 26.
Vajracharya, Vidyaharsha	*Shri Deva devata Stotra Samgraha,* Sanskrit hymnical verses of various deities, Ashoka Manda Pashthana

	Surata Shri Mahavihar, Asantol Takshabahal, Kathmandu, 1935. p. 26.
Vrihat Svayambhu Puranam	*'Containing the traditions of the Svayambhu Kshetra in Nepal'*, edited by Pandit Hara Prasad Shastri M.A. i. Bibliotheca Indica: A collection of oriental works published by the Asiatic Society of Bengal, New series, No. 837. ii. Calcutta, 1894. iii. Baptist Mission Press. iv. Text p. 502, and index p. 38. v. The Original MSS is dated Nepal Era 919.

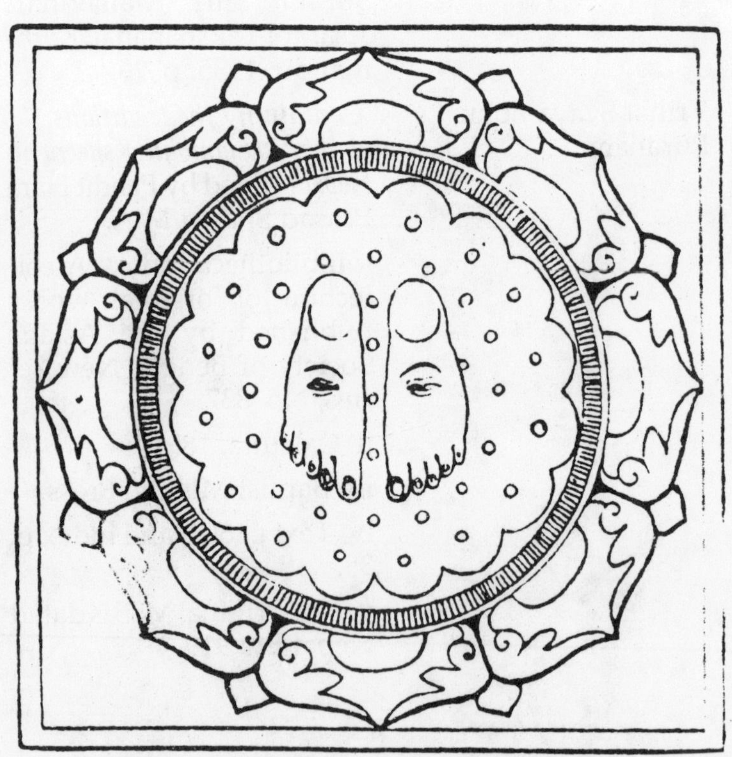

Footsteps of God Manjushri on stone at Swayambhu

God Manjushri

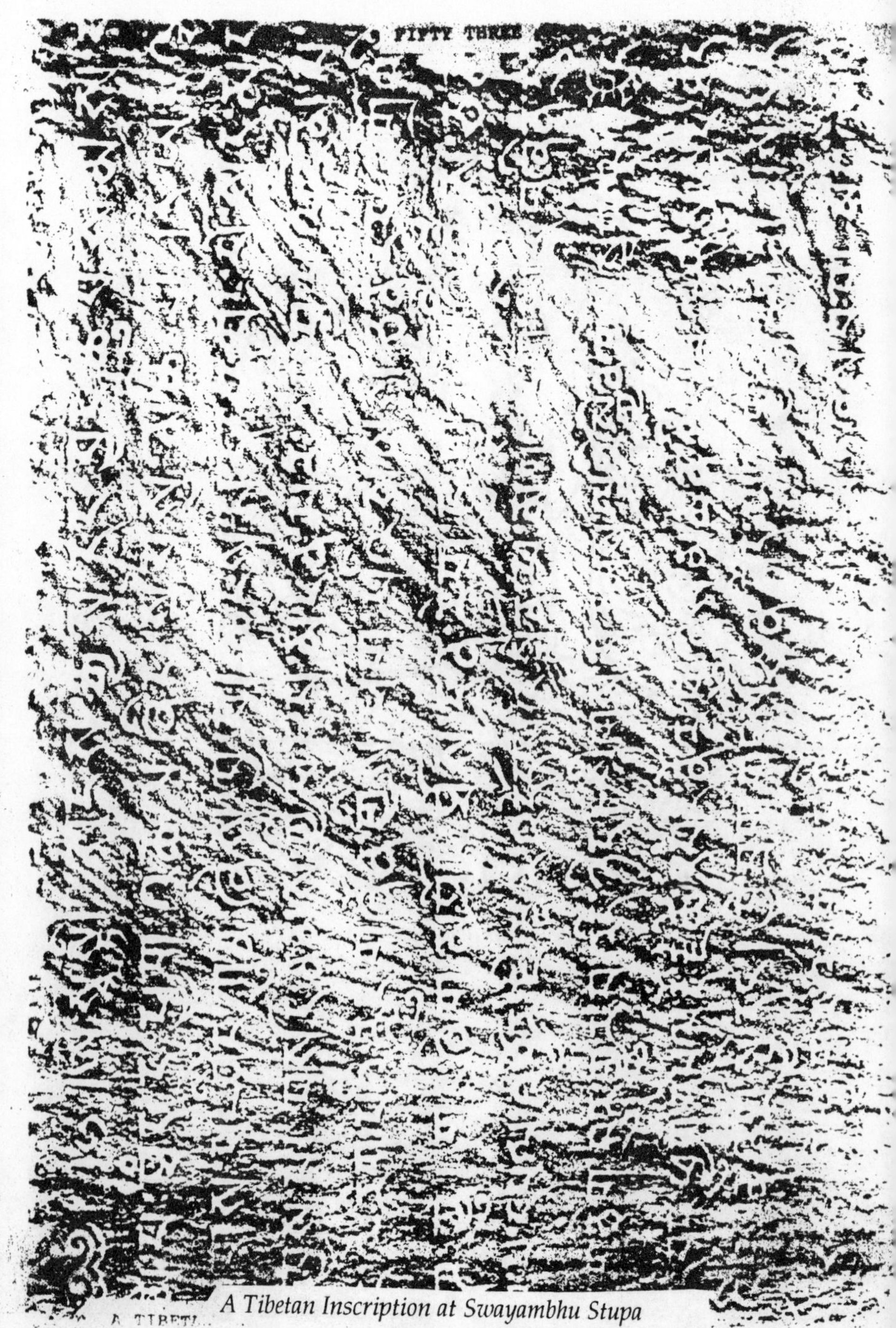

A Tibetan Inscription at Swayambhu Stupa

रिशा चतुरस्रा कार्णविशिरवा चिन्त्यते भावयायं तालि वीतिराख्यानां चतुर्भिर्गृहस्थभिक्षु गेहे सर्वा कृत्वा। तन्मध्ये महा
[illegible]पल्लवी नीमैतालक्षणा नंकृता हरण पञ्च पताक ध्वजाभ्यन्तं कृत सुधालेपितं च्चैत्य राजो विहारेति श्रीमन्मह
[illegible]वहारीयं तन्कर्मणा जाभिषं तीभिक्षु यं यणवि जनतया [illegible] विधान ता विधीयमानो भाषयातन्यवा चि वाहारीति षिंध्यो तो
[illegible]न्व पिशाधुसाधि दिवदेवी परिहत ता। ॥ अथ तयो बुद्धादीनां नाम संख्यानादि कं लिख्यते। तत्र प्रथम तावत् गर्भस्थिते
[illegible]त्पन्न। नदि॥ [illegible] वस्तु धर्मधातु नाम [illegible] ज्ञान प्रवृत्त्यर्थी समुत्पत्तिः १ यस्य नामवर्ण चतु
रिति वि[illegible] सर्वरा सपत्ता नवर्ण चतुर्नामा महाबुद्ध इति नाम २ यस्य भुवनं अकनिष्ठाख्यं सर्व भुवनानामुप
रि [illegible] कनिष्ठं तत् कस्यापि कनिष्ठं न सर्वप्रपञ्च वर्जत्वाद् इति भुवनं ३ यः एकवक्त्रः श्वेतवर्णः द्विभुज उभौ
धर्मचक्रमुद्राधर यस्या मुद्रायां धर्मचक्र संसार समूह [illegible] सम्मूढ़ः पद्मासनः इति ध्यानं सर्वापि[illegible]

तान्यां रूप्य दर्शनमादर्शयंतीय एक मुद्रा भवणा [illegible] देवमाल्यालंकृत पद्मवज्रासना १ तस्या दक्षे वज्रवीणा देवी एकमुख
हि[illegible] वर्णा द्विभुजा वीणां वादयन्ती [illegible]मुद्रालंकृता पद्मवज्रासनः २ अथ वामपार्श्वे अक्षयमति
[illegible] धर्मत्व अक्षोभ्यात् समुत्पन्न [illegible] भुवनं एकमुख [illegible] वर्णा द्विभुज दक्षेण [illegible] वाम[illegible]
याद्वामेन [illegible] कमल विभ्राणः [illegible] कृतः पद्मवज्रासन अक्षोभ्यस्य अक्षयाकार [illegible]
सं १ तस्य वामे [illegible] भद्रनामा [illegible] धर्मत्वः [illegible] समुत्पन्नः भुवनम[illegible] एकमुख श्वेतवर्ण द्विभुज दक्षेण
[illegible] वामे [illegible] विभ्राणा [illegible] भरणालंकृत पद्मवज्रासनप्र
[illegible] सम्यग् २ तस्य वाम [illegible] नाम देवी एकमुख हेमवर्णा द्विभुज [illegible]
[illegible] कृतः पद्मवज्रासनः १ तस्या वामे [illegible] नाम देवी एकमुख [illegible] वर्णा द्विभुज दक्षे

क्रांगरुद्धिभु·पेयाल्नं·सर्पपुछ·पंचवर्षिकंवाल्नं॥५॥ बिडालग्रहः शकुनिग्रहः॥ पश्चिमुख ध्यक्ष·एकं द्विभुज पे
याल्नं सर्पपुछ·पाञ्चवर्षिकंवाल्नं ६ अष्ठतिकग्रहः॥ एकास्य·ध्यक्ष·भूभंगव्यात्ताकंकाल·करुद्विभु·पेयाल्नं
व्याघ्रचर्मी·षट्वर्षिकंवाल्नं ७ जंभूकग्रहः फेरवास्य ध्यक्ष·कर्ध्र्व खर्पर·मेगादि पेयाल्नंअष्टवार्षिकंवाल्नं॥ ८
लोकग्रहः॥ श्वानास्य·ध्यक्ष·एकं·वक्रि·पेयाल्नं नववा० ९ रेवतीग्रहः॥ व्यात्तास्य·दंष्ट्राकराल·एकं वीभत्स·पयभूष
व्याघ्रचर्मो·द्विभु·पेयाल्नं चतुष्पद·दशवर्षिकं॥ १० पितृ ग्रह क्षिरास्य·व्यात्ता·दंष्ट्राकराल·एकं द्विभुज पेयाल्न
एकादश वर्षिकं॥ ११ स्कंदग्रहः श्वेतमिरास्य ध्यक्ष एकांग·भुजाद्विबे·याल्नं·द्वादशवार्षिकंवाल्नं त्रासपत्र
१२॥ ॥ततो शान्तिमंगलवलिः॥ ततः पंचदशग्रहः श्रीववासवलि ततश्चतुर्दशग्रहवलिः॥ ततः कालमृत्युवलि
ततो द्वादशग्रहवलिः॥ दशग्रहः दशक्रोधवलि॥ सामेमंगलवलि॥ ततश्चतुर्दशग्रहवलि सर्वरूपवलि·क्रमतएषां

वलीएनेयग्रहाणांध्यानवलिविस्तरमयाश्लिलिखितं॥ ॥ॐ नमो रत्नत्रयाय॥ ॥श्रीमति नेपालमंडलेगोप
च्छाख्यपर्वते विराजमानोस्ति यत्र स्वयंभू धर्मधातुवागीश्वरो निरंजन एकरूपप्रमाणो
ज्योतिरूपो स्वरजनतत्वं॥ तराज्ञादक·श्रीशान्तिकराचार्य विनिर्मितो धाम्परङ्गकृतिलक्षणाख्य·पंचवक्त्रा याल्य
श्चैत्य एजोत्पशोभतःलोकोद्धरणकृत। तस्मादाग्नेयकोणभागेललितपत्तननामा महानगरं वर्तते यत्र श्रीमद
र्यावलोकितेश्वरस्य प्रपादिपाना बोधिसत्वेन प्रतिपालितश्चतुर्वर्णितसाहस्रिकचातुर्वर्णिकप्रजापरिपूर्णा॥ मणि
गल्वमणिकुमारमणिधारामणिमंडपमणिमंगलभट्टिविराजमानः॥ तस्याग्नेयभागे·हृदयदेवनामे वेरूपरागेन प्रब
जितेनविनिर्मितो·हृदयवर्णनामा महाविहारो विराजते॥ यत्र निर्मलबोधिवृत्तिकाविनिर्मितचतुर्दशलक्षणं·तत्कृत
श्रीशाक्यसिंहबुद्धस्वर्णिदेवमनः॥ यस्य चतुःशतसंख्याकाभिक्षुसंघा विलसंति॥ तस्य विहारस्य पश्चिमभागे दक्षिण

न भैरव न हेरुक स्यामीभिनिक प्रतिमा दधानः । तेषां ऊर्ध्वेषि पिवामेति नये दंकं दधानः शब्देन वधिरा जन्मनान्कापे मीति
दमरुकं दधानः ब्रह्मणां च कालकलनार्थं खट्वांगं बिभ्राणः तदा एष तदा न ब्रह्मणो [illegible] संगता तिसांप्रदायिक
अतो वज्रशासन रक्षणार्थं समस्तकाल [illegible] स्थापिता तथापनीयाश्च । १३ तत्राणां कारणा
पूर्वापरि बुद्धस्य नामादि । एकवक्त्रः श्वेतवर्ण आननयनः [illegible] नामात्नं काएलं कृतम
[illegible] प्रथमाभ्यां सव्यदक्षाभ्यां हृदय प्रदेशे अभयमुद्राद्वयं दयाभ्यां [illegible]
[illegible] सव्यचतुर्थं [illegible] सव्यवाम पंचमाभ्यां पात्र [illegible]
क्षेपणमुद्रा [illegible] नामाभ्यां सपात्र [illegible] वामतृतीये न स वज्र [illegible] खट्वांगं दधानः कमलोपरि [illegible] आसनः
अस्यं नामसंगीति नाम वज्रो भगवान् । गगने [illegible] ॥ ॥ कारणं । [illegible]

[illegible] नामसंगीति नामा बभूव
[illegible] नामसंगीति [illegible] ॥ १४ ॥ देवानामहोरात्र [illegible] मनुष्याणामेक वर्षं [illegible]
[illegible] वर्षं । सत्ययुग प्रमाणं ॥ ॥ षोडश लक्ष प्रमाणं त्रेतायुगं ॥ अष्टालक्ष प्रमाणं द्वा
परयुगं ॥ ॥ चतुर्लक्ष प्रमाणं कलियुगं ॥ ॥ एकसप्तति युगभ्रमणानंतरं प्रलयः ॥ प्रलय [illegible] महाप्रलय
॥ महाप्रलय [illegible] ॥ ॥ तत्र दक्षे स्थित [illegible] एकवक्त्र भीमवज्र [illegible] त्रिनेत्रा भ्रूभंग
कुटिलः [illegible] पंचनागविभूषि
तः [illegible] मुंडमालाधरः व्याघ्रचर्मांबरः द्विभुजः दक्षेण प्रसारितेन [illegible] वज्रं दधानः वामेनाध
[illegible] मार दुष्ट निवारणार्थं भीमन [illegible]

णा॥ मनोमेव प्रकृष्टं ज्ञायते वा आदि भवायां मोक्षता आदि प्रज्ञाः ॥ निरंजना ॥ निर्गतं अंजनं·
पूर्ववत्॥ निराकार॥ निरानया: निर्विकल्पा निराकाशा नित्यादित्या प्रज्ञा प्रज्ञापारमिता: प्रा
प्रज्ञानेन· प्रज्ञायां वा पारं इतार्थात ॥ नैरात्म्या निर्गत आत्मा यस्या· सा· ··· तत्सगमनं रहित
त्वात्॥ ॥ नैरज·· ·· निर्गतानि अवयवानि यस्याः पंचज्ञानेन्द्रियत्वात्· ज्ञायते॥ ॥
त्रिकोणाकार:॥ शून्यभवनं त्रिकोणां अस्य आकारं रूपं शून्यभुवनं· प्रज्ञोस॥ १॥ ॥आ
नाकार॥ एतादृश्-इति रूपरहित आकारो यस्या २ चातुर्युगीया आद्यनुत्पन्नत्वात्॥युगरहि
ताव· यतो युगादय: ३ सार्वकार्मिका॥ कर्मणा· हीनत्वात्· यत: कर्मणां संभवं ···प्रहीनं कार्य॥
··स्या: सकाशात् संभवत:॥ ४॥ निपुणा॥ निर्गत आत्मा सा तत्पगमनं हीनत्वात्॥ ५॥ ॥प्रज्ञोपा

···येः संमीलनात्· आम्नायानां बुद्ध धर्म संघानां नामादिकं॥ ॥बुद्धस्य॥ ॥बुद्ध:॥ बोधनात्म
बुद्ध: स्वयं बुद्धा परान् बोधयति· प्रज्ञोपायमीलने नेति॥ ॥सर्वज्ञ:॥ लौकिकं लोकान्तरं ज्ञानात्मि
कत्वात् सर्वज्ञानमय:॥ ॥सुगत:॥ स्वयं सुगतेन निर्वाणे स्थित्वा लोकान् ज्ञापयिता॥ ॥ध
राजा॥ धर्मो राजा· धर्मोपार्जनेन संसारे राजनं धर्मो राजते यस्मात्· धर्ममय चातुर्युगीया:॥ ॥त
गत:॥ तथा तत्रैव प्रशुगमागत्वा निर्वृतिं गत:॥ ॥समंतभद्र:॥ समंततो भद्रं यस्मात्॥ ॥
भगवान्॥ भगं नाम षट्के: श्रेयं नहि इति· कामं भंजयन् मारादित्यादि ॥ मारजित्॥ मारं तु मारं
···जित इति॥ ॥लोकजित्॥ लोकं यंतीति लोकाः तान् जयति· वा लोकान् भुवनानि॥ ॥जिन·
प्रहीनं निहत्य योनं यद्वीजो जिन:॥ ॥षडभिज्ञ:॥ षड् अभिज्ञा यस्मिन्· अभिसर्वतो भावेन ज्ञा

Nirala Series

A Series of Contemporary Writing

1. ***The Gurkhas***
   A History of the Recruitment in the British Indian Army
   Kamal Raj Singh Rathaur
2. ***The Khasa Kingdom***
   A Trans Himalayan Empire of the Middle Age
   Surya Mani Adhikary
3. ***Sources of Inflation in Asia***
   Theory and Evidences
   Raghab D. Pant
4. ***The Sherpas : Fire of Himal***
   An Anthropological Study of the Sherpas of Nepal Himalayan Region
   Ramesh Raj Kunwar
5. ***A Macro-economic Study of the Nepalese Plan Performance***
   Gunanidhi Sharma
6. ***Folk Culture of Nepal***
   An Analytical Study
   Ram Dayal Rakesh
7. ***Fundamentals of Library and Information Science***
   A Nepalese Response
   Madhusudan Sharma Subedi
8. ***Transit of Land-locked Countries and Nepal***
   Gajendra Mani Pradhan
9. ***The Gurungs: Thunder of Himal***
   A Cross-cultural Study of a Nepalese Ethnic Group
   Murari P. Regmi
10. ***Folk Tales of Sherpa and Yeti***

Shiva Dhakal

11. ***Gods and Mountains: The Folk Culture of a Himalayan Kingdom: Nepal***
Kesar Lall

12. ***Art and Culture of Nepal***
An Attempt towards Preservation
Saphalya Amatya

13. ***The Dhimals: Miraculous Migrants of Himal***
An Anthropoligical Study of a Nepalese Ethnic Group
Rishikeshab Raj Regmi

14. ***Sales Promotion in Nepal***
Policies and Practices
Parashar Prasad Koirala

15. ***Glimpses of Tourism, Airlines and Management in Nepal***
B.R. Singh

16. ***The Taming of Tibet***
A Historical Account of Compromise and Confrontation in Nepal-Tibet Relations (1900-193)
Tirtha Prasad Mishra

17. ***Dolpo***
The Hidden Paradise
A Journey to the Endangered Sanctury of the Himalayan Kingdom of Nepal
Karna Sakya

18. ***Secrets of Shangri-la***
An Inquiry into the Lore, Legend and Culture of Nepal
Nagendra Sharma

19. ***Transportation Systems in Nepal***
Mukund R. Satyal

20. ***Indo-Nepal Trade Relations***

A Historical Analysis of Nepal's Trade with the British India
Shri Ram Upadhyaya

21. ***Politics and Development in Nepal:***
Some Issues
Narayan Khadka

22. ***The Gurkha Connection***
A History of Gorkha Recruitment in the British Army
Purshottam Baskota

23. ***Lore and Legend of the Kathmandu Valley***
Shiva Dhakal

24. ***Recent Nepal***
The Analysis of the Recent Democratic Upsurge and its Aftermath
Laksman Bahadur K.C.

25. ***Popular Deities Emblems and Images of Nepal***
Dhruba K. Deep

26. ***The Cultural Heritage of Nepal Terai***
Ram Dayal Rakesh

27. ***The Nepala-mahatmya***
Legends of the Sacred Places and Deities of Nepal
Jayaraj Acharya

28. ***A Glossary of Himalayan Buddhism***
Jagadish Chandra Regmi

29. ***Kathmandu, Patan &Bhakatapur***
An Archaelogical Anthropology of the Royal Cities of the Kathmandu Valley
Rishikeshab R. Regmi

30. ***Contemporary Psychology in Nepal***
Murari P. Regmi

31. ***Wild Life and Conservation in Nepal***

Rishikesh Shah & Richard M. Mitchell

32. ***Politics of Himalayan River Waters***
An Analysis of the River Water
Issues of Nepal, India and Bangladesh
B.C. Uprety

33. ***The Nepali Congress***
An Analysis of the Party's Performance in the General Elections and its Aftermath
B.C. Uprety

34. ***The Chepangs***
Ganesh Gurung

35. ***Folktales of Nepal***
Yuyutsu R.D. Sharma

36. ***Nepal-India***
Democracy in the Making of Mutual Trust
Dinesh Bhattarai & Pradip Khatiwada

37. ***Making of Modern Nepal***
Ram Niwas Pandey

38. ***Encounter Wild Life in Nepal***
Karna Sakya

39. ***Constitutional Monarchy and Parliamentary Democracy in Nepal***
Laksman Bahadur K.C.

40. ***Festivals of Nepal***
Hemanta Kumar Jha